The Autobiography of an Ex-Colored Man
by James Weldon Johnson

Wilder Publications, LLC.
PO Box 3005
Radford VA 24143-3005

ISBN 10: 1-60459-217-6
ISBN 13: 978-1-60459-217-7

PREFACE

This vivid and startlingly new picture of conditions brought about by the race question in the United States makes no special plea for the Negro, but shows in a dispassionate, though sympathetic, manner conditions as they actually exist between the whites and blacks to-day. Special pleas have already been made for and against the Negro in hundreds of books, but in these books either his virtues or his vices have been exaggerated. This is because writers, in nearly every instance, have treated the colored American as a whole; each has taken some one group of the race to prove his case. Not before has a composite and proportionate presentation of the entire race, embracing all of its various groups and elements, showing their relations with each other and to the whites, been made.

It is very likely that the Negroes of the United States have a fairly correct idea of what the white people of the country think of them, for that opinion has for a long time been and is still being constantly stated; but they are themselves more or less a sphinx to the whites. It is curiously interesting and even vitally important to know what are the thoughts of ten millions of them concerning the people among whom they live. In these pages it is as though a veil had been drawn aside: the reader is given a view of the inner life of the Negro in America, is initiated into the "free-masonry," as it were, of the race.

These pages also reveal the unsuspected fact that prejudice against the Negro is exerting a pressure, which, in New York and other large cities where the opportunity is open, is actually and constantly forcing an unascertainable number of fair-complexioned colored people over into the white race.

In this book the reader is given a glimpse behind the scenes of this race-drama which is being here enacted,—he is taken upon an elevation where he can catch a bird's-eye view of the conflict which is being waged.

The Publishers

CHAPTER I

I know that in writing the following pages I am divulging the great secret of my life, the secret which for some years I have guarded far more carefully than any of my earthly possessions; and it is a curious study to me to analyze the motives which prompt me to do it. I feel that I am led by the same impulse which forces the unfound-out criminal to take somebody into his confidence, although he knows that the act is liable, even almost certain, to lead to his undoing. I know that I am playing with fire, and I feel the thrill which accompanies that most fascinating pastime; and, back of it all, I think I find a sort of savage and diabolical desire to gather up all the little tragedies of my life, and turn them into a practical joke on society.

And, too, I suffer a vague feeling of unsatisfaction, of regret, of almost remorse from which I am seeking relief, and of which I shall speak in the last paragraph of this account.

I was born in a little town of Georgia a few years after the close of the Civil War. I shall not mention the name of the town, because there are people still living there who could be connected with this narrative. I have only a faint recollection of the place of my birth. At times I can close my eyes, and call up in a dream-like way things that seem to have happened ages ago in some other world. I can see in this half vision a little house,—I am quite sure it was not a large one;—I can remember that flowers grew in the front yard, and that around each bed of flowers was a hedge of vari-colored glass bottles stuck in the ground neck down. I remember that once, while playing around in the sand, I became curious to know whether or not the bottles grew as the flowers did, and I proceeded to dig them up to find out; the investigation brought me a terrific spanking which indelibly fixed the incident in my mind. I can remember, too, that behind the house was a shed under which stood two or three wooden wash-tubs. These tubs were the earliest aversion of my life, for regularly on certain evenings I was plunged into one of them, and scrubbed until my skin ached. I can remember to this day the pain caused by the strong, rank soap getting into my eyes.

Back from the house a vegetable garden ran, perhaps, seventy-five or one hundred feet; but to my childish fancy it was an endless territory. I can still recall the thrill of joy, excitement and wonder it gave me to go on an exploring expedition through it, to find the blackberries, both ripe and green, that grew along the edge of the fence.

I remember with what pleasure I used to arrive at, and stand before, a little enclosure in which stood a patient cow chewing her cud, how I would occasionally offer her through the bars a piece of my bread and molasses, and how I would jerk back my hand in half fright if she made any motion to accept my offer.

I have a dim recollection of several people who moved in and about this little house, but I have a distinct mental image of only two; one, my mother, and the other, a tall man with a small, dark mustache. I remember that his shoes or boots were always shiny, and that he wore a gold chain and a great gold watch with which he was always willing to let me play. My admiration was almost equally divided between the watch and chain and the shoes. He used to come to the house evenings, perhaps two or three times a week; and it became my appointed duty whenever he came to bring him a pair of slippers, and to put the shiny shoes in a particular corner; he often gave me in return for this service a bright coin which my mother taught me to promptly drop in a little tin bank. I remember distinctly the last time this tall man came to the little house in Georgia; that evening before I went to bed he took me up in his arms, and squeezed me very tightly; my mother stood behind his chair wiping tears from her eyes. I remember how I sat upon his knee, and watched him laboriously drill a hole through a ten-dollar gold piece, and then tie the coin around my neck with a string. I have worn that gold piece around my neck the greater part of my life, and still possess it, but more than once I have wished that some other way had been found of attaching it to me besides putting a hole through it.

On the day after the coin was put around my neck my mother and I started on what seemed to me an endless journey. I knelt on the seat and watched through the train window the corn and cotton fields pass swiftly by until I fell asleep. When I fully awoke we were being driven through the streets of a large city—Savannah. I sat up and blinked at the bright lights. At Savannah we boarded a steamer which finally landed us in New York. From New York we went to a town in Connecticut, which became the home of my boyhood.

My mother and I lived together in a little cottage which seemed to me to be fitted up almost luxuriously; there were horse-hair covered chairs in the parlor, and a little square piano; there was a stairway with red carpet on it leading to a half second story; there were pictures on the walls, and a few books in a glass-doored case. My mother dressed me very neatly, and I developed that pride which well-dressed boys generally have. She was careful about my associates, and I myself was quite particular. As I look back now I can see that I was a perfect little aristocrat. My mother rarely went to anyone's house, but she did sewing, and there were a great many ladies coming to our cottage. If I were around they would generally call me, and ask me my name and age and tell my mother what a pretty boy I was. Some of them would pat me on the head and kiss me.

My mother was kept very busy with her sewing; sometimes she would have another woman helping her. I think she must have derived a fair income from her work. I know, too, that at least once each month she received a letter; I used to watch for the postman, get the letter, and run to her with it; whether she was busy or not she would take it and instantly thrust it into her bosom. I never saw her read one of them. I knew later that these letters contained money and, what was to her, more than money. As busy as she generally was she, however, found time to teach me my letters and figures and how to spell a number of easy words. Always on Sunday evenings she opened the little square piano, and picked out hymns. I can recall now that whenever she played hymns from the book her tempos were always decidedly largo. Sometimes on other evenings when she was not sewing she would play simple accompaniments to some old southern songs which she sang. In these songs she was freer, because she played them by ear. Those evenings on which she opened the little piano were the happiest hours of my childhood. Whenever she started toward the instrument I used to follow her with all the interest and irrepressible joy that a pampered pet dog shows when a package is opened in which he knows there is a sweet bit for him. I used to stand by her side, and often interrupt and annoy her by chiming in with strange harmonies which I found either on the high keys of the treble or low keys of the bass. I remember that I had a particular fondness for the black keys. Always on such evenings, when the music was over, my mother would sit with me in her arms often for a very long time. She would hold me close, softly crooning some old melody without words, all the while gently stroking her face against my head; many and many a night I thus fell asleep. I can see her now, her great dark eyes looking into the fire, to where? No one knew but she. The memory of that picture has more than once kept me from straying too far from the place of purity and safety in which her arms held me.

At a very early age I began to thump on the piano alone, and it was not long before I was able to pick out a few tunes. When I was seven years old I could play by ear all of the hymns and songs that my mother knew. I had also learned the names of the notes in both clefs, but I preferred not to be hampered by notes. About this time several ladies for whom my mother sewed heard me play, and they persuaded her that I should at once be put under a teacher; so arrangements were made for me to study the piano with a lady who was a fairly good musician; at the same time arrangements were made for me to study my books with this lady's daughter. My music teacher had no small difficulty at first in pinning me down to the notes. If she played my lesson over for me I invariably attempted to reproduce the required sounds without the slightest recourse to the written characters. Her daughter, my other teacher, also had her worries. She found that, in reading, whenever I came to words that were difficult or unfamiliar I was prone to bring my imagination to the rescue and read from the picture. She has laughingly told me, since then, that I would sometimes substitute whole sentences and even paragraphs from what meaning I thought the illustrations conveyed. She said she sometimes was not only amused at the fresh treatment I would give an author's subject, but that when I gave some new and sudden turn to the plot of the story she often grew interested and even excited in listening to hear what kind of a denouement I would bring about. But I am sure this was not due to dullness, for I made rapid progress in both my music and my books.

And so, for a couple of years my life was divided between my music and my school books. Music took up the greater part of my time. I had no playmates, but amused myself with games—some of them my own invention—which could be played alone. I knew a few boys whom I had met at the church which I attended with my mother, but I had formed no close friendships with any of them. Then, when I was nine years old, my mother decided to enter me in the public school, so all at once I found myself thrown among a crowd of boys of all sizes and kinds; some of them seemed to me like savages. I shall never forget the bewilderment, the pain, the heart-sickness of that first day at school. I seemed to be the only stranger in the place; every other boy seemed to know every other boy. I was fortunate enough, however, to be assigned to a teacher who knew me; my mother made her dresses. She was one of the ladies who used to pat me on the head and kiss me. She had the tact to address a few words directly to me; this gave me a certain sort of standing in the class, and put me somewhat at ease.

Within a few days I had made one staunch friend, and was on fairly good terms with most of the boys. I was shy of the girls, and remained so; even now, a word or look from a pretty woman sets me all a-tremble. This friend I bound to me with hooks of steel in a very simple way. He was a big awkward boy with a face full of freckles and a head full of very red hair. He was perhaps fourteen years of age; that is, four or five years older than any other boy in the class. This seniority was due to the fact that he had spent twice the required amount of time in several of the preceding classes. I had not been at school many hours before I felt that "Red Head"—as I involuntarily called him—and I were to be friends. I do not doubt that this feeling was strengthened by the fact that I had been quick enough to see that a big, strong boy was a friend to be desired at a public school; and, perhaps, in spite of his dullness, "Red Head" had been able to discern that I could be of service to him. At any rate there was a simultaneous mutual attraction.

The teacher had strung the class promiscuously round the walls of the room for a sort of trial heat for places of rank; when the line was straightened out I found that by skillful maneuvering I had placed myself third, and had piloted "Red Head" to the place next to me. The teacher began by giving us to spell the words corresponding to our order in the line. "Spell first." "Spell second." "Spell third." I rattled off, "t-h-i-r-d, third," in a way which said, "Why don't you give us something hard?" As the words went down the line I could see how lucky I had been to get a good place together with an easy word. As young as I was I felt impressed with the unfairness of the whole proceeding when I saw the tailenders going down before "twelfth" and "twentieth," and I felt sorry for those who had to spell such words in order to hold a low position. "Spell fourth." "Red Head," with his hands clutched tightly behind his back, began bravely, "f-o-r-t-h." Like a flash a score of hands went up, and the teacher began saying, "No snapping of fingers, no snapping of fingers." This was the first word missed, and it seemed to me that some of the scholars were about to lose their senses; some were dancing up and down on one foot with a hand above their heads, the fingers working furiously, and joy beaming all over their faces; others stood still, their hands raised not so high, their fingers working less rapidly, and their faces expressing not quite so much happiness; there were still others who did not move nor raise their hands, but stood with great wrinkles on their foreheads, looking very thoughtful.

The whole thing was new to me, and I did not raise my hand, but slyly whispered the letter "u" to "Red Head" several times. "Second chance," said the teacher. The hands went down and the class became quiet. "Red Head," his face now red, after looking beseechingly at the ceiling, then pitiably at the floor, began very haltingly, "f-u-." Immediately an impulse to raise hands went through the class, but the teacher checked it, and poor "Red Head," though he knew that each letter he added only took him farther out of the way, went doggedly on and finished, "r-t-h." The hand raising was now repeated with more hubbub and excitement than at first. Those who before had not moved a finger were now waving their hands above their heads. "Red Head" felt that he was lost. He looked very big and foolish, and some of the scholars began to snicker. His helpless condition went straight to my heart, and gripped my sympathies. I felt that if he failed it would in some way be my failure. I raised my hand, and under cover of the excitement and the teacher's attempts to regain order, I hurriedly shot up into his ear twice, quite distinctly, "f-o-u-r-t-h," "f-o-u-r-t-h." The teacher tapped on her desk and said, "Third and last chance." The hands came down, the silence became oppressive. "Red Head" began, "f"— Since that day I have waited anxiously for many a turn of the wheel of fortune, but never under greater tension than I watched for the order in which those letters would fall from "Red's" lips—"o-u-r-t-h." A sigh of relief and disappointment went up from the class. Afterwards, through all our school days, "Red Head" shared my wit and quickness and I benefited by his strength and dogged faithfulness.

There were some black and brown boys and girls in the school, and several of them were in my class. One of the boys strongly attracted my attention from the first day I saw him. His face was as black as night, but shone as though it was polished; he had sparkling eyes, and when he opened his mouth he displayed glistening white teeth. It struck me at once as appropriate to call him "Shiny face," or "Shiny eyes," or "Shiny teeth," and I spoke of him often by one of these names to the other boys. These terms were finally merged into "Shiny," and to that name he answered good naturedly during the balance of his public school days.

"Shiny" was considered without question to be the best speller, the best reader, the best penman, in a word, the best scholar, in the class. He was very quick to catch anything; but, nevertheless, studied hard; thus he possessed two powers very rarely combined in one boy. I saw him year after year, on up into the high school, win the majority of the prizes for punctuality, deportment, essay writing and declamation. Yet it did not take me long to discover that, in spite of his standing as a scholar, he was in some way looked down upon.

The other black boys and girls were still more looked down upon. Some of the boys often spoke of them as "niggers." Sometimes on the way home from school a crowd would walk behind them repeating:

"Nigger, nigger, never die,
Black face and shiny eye."

On one such afternoon one of the black boys turned suddenly on his tormentors, and hurled a slate; it struck one of the white boys in the mouth, cutting a slight gash in his lip. At sight of the blood the boy who had thrown the slate ran, and his companions quickly followed. We ran after them pelting them with stones until they separated in several directions. I was very much wrought up over the affair, and went home and told my mother how one of the "niggers" had struck a boy with a slate. I shall never forget how she turned on me. "Don't you ever use that word again," she said, "and don't you ever bother the colored children at school. You ought to be ashamed of yourself." I did hang my head in shame, but not because she had convinced me that I had done wrong, but because I was hurt by the first sharp word she had ever given me.

My school days ran along very pleasantly. I stood well in my studies, not always so well with regard to my behavior. I was never guilty of any serious misconduct, but my love of fun sometimes got me into trouble. I remember, however, that my sense of humor was so sly that most of the trouble usually fell on the head of the other fellow. My ability to play on the piano at school exercises was looked upon as little short of marvelous in a boy of my age. I was not chummy with many of my mates, but, on the whole, was about as popular as it is good for a boy to be.

One day near the end of my second term at school the principal came into our room, and after talking to the teacher, for some reason said, "I wish all of the white scholars to stand for a moment." I rose with the others. The teacher looked at me, and calling my name said, "You sit down for the present, and rise with the others." I did not quite understand her, and questioned, "Ma'm?" She repeated with a softer tone in her voice, "You sit down now, and rise with the others." I sat down dazed. I saw and heard nothing. When the others were asked to rise I did not know it. When school was dismissed I went out in a kind of stupor. A few of the white boys jeered me, saying, "Oh, you're a nigger too." I heard some black children say, "We knew he was colored." "Shiny" said to them, "Come along, don't tease him," and thereby won my undying gratitude.

I hurried on as fast as I could, and had gone some distance before I perceived that "Red Head" was walking by my side. After a while he said to me, "Le' me carry your books." I gave him my strap without being able to answer. When we got to my gate he said as he handed me my books, "Say, you know my big red agate? I can't shoot with it any more. I'm going to bring it to school for you to-morrow." I took my books and ran into the house. As I passed through the hallway I saw that my mother was busy with one of her customers; I rushed up into my own little room, shut the door, and went quickly to where my looking-glass hung on the wall. For an instant I was afraid to look, but when I did I looked long and earnestly. I had often heard people say to my mother, "What a pretty boy you have." I was accustomed to hear remarks about my beauty; but, now, for the first time, I became conscious of it, and recognized it. I noticed the ivory whiteness of my skin, the beauty of my mouth, the size and liquid darkness of my eyes, and how the long black lashes that fringed and shaded them produced an effect that was strangely fascinating even to me. I noticed the softness and glossiness of my dark hair that fell in waves over my temples, making my forehead appear whiter than it really was. How long I stood there gazing at my image I do not know. When I came out and reached the head of the stairs, I heard the lady who had been with my mother going out. I ran downstairs, and rushed to where my mother was sitting with a piece of work in her hands. I buried my head in her lap and blurted out, "Mother, mother, tell me, am I a nigger?" I could not see her face, but I knew the piece of work dropped to the floor, and I felt her hands on my head. I looked up into her face and repeated, "Tell me, mother, am I a nigger?" There were tears in her eyes, and I could see that she was suffering for me. And then it was that I looked at her critically for the first time. I had thought of her in a childish way only as the most beautiful woman in the world; now I looked at her searching for defects. I could see that her skin was almost brown, that her hair was not so soft as mine, and that she did differ in some way from the other ladies who came to the house; yet, even so, I could see that she was very beautiful, more beautiful than any of them. She must have felt that I was examining her, for she hid her face in my hair, and said with difficulty, "No, my darling, you are not a nigger." She went on, "You are as good as anybody; if anyone calls you a nigger don't notice them." But the more she talked the less was I reassured, and I stopped her by asking, "Well, mother, am I white? Are you white?" She answered tremblingly, "No, I am not white, but you—your father is one of the greatest men in the country—the best blood of the South is in you—" This suddenly opened up in my heart a fresh chasm of misgiving and fear, and I almost fiercely demanded, "Who is my father? Where is he?" She stroked my hair and said, "I'll tell you about him some day." I sobbed, "I want to know now." She answered, "No, not now."

Perhaps it had to he done, but I have never forgiven the woman who did it so cruelly. It may be that she never knew that she gave me a sword-thrust that day in school which was years in healing.

CHAPTER II

Since I have grown older I have often gone back and tried to analyze the change that came into my life after that fateful day in school. There did come a radical change, and, young as I was, I felt fully conscious of it, though I did not fully comprehend it. Like my first spanking, it is one of the few incidents in my life that I can remember clearly. In the life of every one there is a limited number of unhappy experiences which are not written upon the memory, but stamped there with a die; and in long years after they can be called up in detail, and every emotion that was stirred by them can he lived through anew; these are the tragedies of life. We may grow to include some of them among the trivial incidents of childhood—a broken toy, a promise made to us which was not kept, a harsh, heart-piercing word—but these, too, as well as the bitter experiences and disappointments of mature years, are the tragedies of life.

And so I have often lived through that hour, that day, that week in which was wrought the miracle of my transition from one world into another; for I did indeed pass into another world. From that time I looked out through other eyes, my thoughts were colored, my words dictated, my actions limited by one dominating, all-pervading idea which constantly increased in force and weight until I finally realized in it a great, tangible fact.

And this is the dwarfing, warping, distorting influence which operates upon each colored man in the United States. He is forced to take his outlook on all things, not from the viewpoint of a citizen, or a man, nor even a human being, but from the viewpoint of a colored man. It is wonderful to me that the race has progressed so broadly as it has, since most of its thought and all of its activity must run through the narrow neck of one funnel.

And it is this, too, which makes the colored people of this country, in reality, a mystery to the whites. It is a difficult thing for a white man to learn what a colored man really thinks; because, generally, with the latter an additional and different light must be brought to bear on what he thinks; and his thoughts are often influenced by considerations so delicate and subtle that it would be impossible for him to confess or explain them to one of the opposite race. This gives to every colored man, in proportion to his intellectuality, a sort of dual personality; there is one phase of him which is disclosed only in the freemasonry of his own race. I have often watched with interest and sometimes with amazement even ignorant colored men under cover of broad grins and minstrel antics maintain this dualism in the presence of white men.

I believe it to be a fact that the colored people of this country know and understand the white people better than the white people know and understand them.

I now think that this change which came into niy life was at first more subjective than objective. I do not think my friends at school changed so much toward me as I did toward them. I grew reserved, I might say suspicious. I grew constantly more and more afraid of laying myself open to some injury to my feelings or my pride. I frequently saw or fancied some slight where, I am sure, none was intended. On the other hand, my friends and teachers were, if anything different, more considerate of me; but I can remember that it was against this very attitude in particular that my sensitiveness revolted. "Red" was the only one who did not so wound me; up to this day I recall with a swelling heart his clumsy efforts to make me understand that nothing could change his love for me.

I am sure that at this time the majority of my white schoolmates did not understand or appreciate any differences between me and themselves; but there were a few who had evidently received instructions at home on the matter, and more than once they displayed their knowledge in word and action. As the years passed I noticed that the most innocent and ignorant among the others grew in wisdom.

I, myself, would not have so clearly understood this difference had it not been for the presence of the other colored children at school; I had. learned what their status was, and now I learned that theirs was mine. I had had no particular like or dislike for these black and brown boys and girls; in fact, with the exception of "Shiny," they had occupied very little of my thought, but I do know that when the blow fell I had a very strong aversion to being classed with them. So I became something of a solitary. "Red" and I remained inseparable, and there was between "Shiny" and me a sort of sympathetic bond, but my intercourse with the others was never entirely free from a feeling of constraint. But I must add that this feeling was confined almost entirely to my intercourse with boys and girls of about my own age; I did not experience it with my seniors. And when I grew to manhood I found myself freer with elderly white people than with those near my own age.

I was now about eleven years old, but these emotions and impressions which I have just described could not have been stronger or more distinct at an older age. There were two immediate results of my forced loneliness; I began to find company in books, and greater pleasure in music. I made the former discovery through a big, gilt-bound, illustrated copy of the Bible, which used to lie in splendid neglect on the center table in our little parlor. On top of the Bible lay a photograph album. I had often looked at the pictures in the album, and one day after taking the larger book down, and opening it on the floor, I was overjoyed to find that it contained what seemed to be an inexhaustible supply of pictures. I looked at these pictures many times; in fact, so often that I knew the story of each one without having to read the subject, and then, somehow, I picked up the thread of history on which is strung the trials and tribulations of the Hebrew children; this I followed with feverish interest and excitement. For a long time King David, with Samson a close second, stood at the head of my list of heroes; he was not displaced until I came to know Robert the Bruce. I read a good portion of the Old Testament, all that part treating of wars and rumors of wars, and then started in on the New. I became interested in the life of Christ, but became impatient and disappointed when I found that, notwithstanding the great power he possessed, he did not make use of it when, in my judgment, he most needed to do so. And so my first general impression of the Bible was what my later impression has been of a number of modern books, that the authors put their best work in the first part, and grew either exhausted or careless toward the end.

After reading the Bible, or those parts which held my attention, I began to explore the glass-doored book-case which I have already mentioned. I found there "Pilgrim's Progress," "Peter Parley's History of the United States," Grimm's "Household Stories," "Tales of a Grandfather," a bound volume of an old English publication, I think it was called "The Mirror," a little volume called "Familiar Science," and somebody's "Natural Theology," which latter, of course, I could not read, but which, nevertheless, I tackled, with the result of gaining a permanent dislike for all kinds of theology. There were several other books of no particular name or merit, such as agents sell to people who know nothing of buying books. How my mother came by this little library which, considering all things, was so well suited to me, I never sought to know. But she was far from being an ignorant woman, and had herself, very likely, read the majority of these books, though I do not remember ever having seen her with a book in her hand, with the exception of the Episcopal Prayer-book. At any rate she encouraged in me the habit of reading, and when I had about exhausted those books in the little library which interested me, she began to buy books for me. She also regularly gave me money to buy a weekly paper which was then very popular for boys.

At this time I went in for music with an earnestness worthy of maturer years; a change of teachers was largely responsible for this. I began now to take lessons of the organist of the church which I attended with my mother; he was a good teacher and quite a thorough musician. He was so skillful in his instruction, and filled me with such enthusiasm that my progress—these are his words—was marvelous. I remember that when I was barely twelve years old I appeared on a program with a number of adults at an entertainment given for some charitable purpose, and carried off the honors. I did more, I brought upon myself through the local newspapers the handicapping title of "Infant prodigy."

I can believe that I did astonish my audience, for I never played the piano like a child, that is, in the "one-two-three" style with accelerated motion. Neither did I depend upon mere brilliancy of technic, a trick by which children often surprise their listeners, but I always tried to interpret a piece of music; I always played with feeling. Very early I acquired that knack of using the pedals which makes the piano a sympathetic, singing instrument; quite a different thing from the source of hard or blurred sounds it so generally is. I think this was due not entirely to natural artistic temperament, but largely to the fact that I did not begin to learn the piano by counting out exercises, but by trying to reproduce the quaint songs which my mother used to sing, with all their pathetic turns and cadences.

Even at a tender age, in playing, I helped to express what I felt by some of the mannerisms which I afterwards observed in great performers; I had not copied them. I have often heard people speak of the mannerisms of musicians as affectations adopted for mere effect; in some cases this may be so; but a true artist can no more play upon the piano or violin without putting his whole body in accord with the emotions he is striving to express than a swallow can fly without being graceful. Often when playing I could not keep the tears which formed in my eyes from rolling down my cheeks. Sometimes at the end or even in the midst of a composition as big a boy as I was, I would jump from the piano, and throw myself sobbing into my mother's arms. She, by her caresses and often her tears, only encouraged these fits of sentimental hysteria. Of course, to counteract this tendency to temperamental excesses I should have been out playing ball or in swimming with other boys of my age; but my mother didn't know that. There was only once when she was really firm with me, making me do what she considered was best; I did not want to return to school after the unpleasant episode which I have related, and she was inflexible.

I began my third term, and the days ran along as I have already indicated. I had been promoted twice, and had managed each time to pull "Red" along with me. I think the teachers came to consider me the only hope of his ever getting through school, and I believe they secretly conspired with me to bring about the desired end. At any rate, I know it became easier in each succeeding examination for me not only to assist "Red," but absolutely to do his work. It is strange how in some things honest people can be dishonest without the slightest compunction. I knew boys at school who were too honorable to tell a fib even when one would have been just the right thing, but could not resist the temptation to assist or receive assistance in an examination. I have long considered it the highest proof of honesty in a man to hand his street-car fare to the conductor who had overlooked it.

One afternoon after school, during my third term, I rushed home in a great hurry to get my dinner, and go to my music teacher's. I was never reluctant about going there, but on this particular afternoon I was impetuous. The reason of this was, I had been asked to play the accompaniment for a young lady who was to play a violin solo at a concert given by the young people of the church, and on this afternoon we were to have our first rehearsal. At that time playing accompaniments was the only thing in music I did not enjoy; later this feeling grew into positive dislike. I have never been a really good accompanist because my ideas of interpretation were always too strongly individual. I constantly forced my accelerandos and rubatos upon the soloist, often throwing the duet entirely out of gear.

Perhaps the reader has already guessed why I was so willing and anxious to play the accompaniment to this violin solo; if not,—the violinist was a girl of seventeen or eighteen whom I had first heard play a short time before on a Sunday afternoon at a special service of some kind, and who had moved me to a degree which now I can hardly think of as possible. At present I do not think it was due to her wonderful playing, though I judge she must have been a very fair performer, but there was just the proper setting to produce the effect upon a boy such as I was; the half dim church, the air of devotion on the part of the listeners, the heaving tremor of the organ under the clear wail of the violin, and she, her eyes almost closing, the escaping strands of her dark hair wildly framing her pale face, and her slender body swaying to the tones she called forth, all combined to fire my imagination and my heart with a passion though boyish, yet strong and, somehow, lasting. I have tried to describe the scene; if I have succeeded it is only half success, for words can only partially express what I would wish to convey. Always in recalling that Sunday afternoon I am subconscious of a faint but distinct fragrance which, like some old memory-awakening perfume, rises and suffuses my whole imagination, inducing a state of reverie so airy as to just evade the powers of expression.

She was my first love, and I loved her as only a boy loves. I dreamed of her, I built air castles for her, she was the incarnation of each beautiful heroine I knew; when I played the piano it was to her, not even did music furnish an adequate outlet for my passion; I bought a new note-book, and, to sing her praises, made my first and last attempts at poetry. I remember one day at school, after having given in our note-books to have some exercises corrected, the teacher called me to her desk and said, "I couldn't correct your exercises because I found nothing in your book but a rhapsody on somebody's brown eyes." I had passed in the wrong note-book. I don't think I have felt greater embarrassment in my whole life than I did at that moment. I was not only ashamed that my teacher should see this nakedness of my heart, but that she should find out that I had any knowledge of such affairs. It did not then occur to me to be ashamed of the kind of poetry I had written.

Of course, the reader must know that all of this adoration was in secret; next to my great love for this young lady was the dread that in some way she would find it out. I did not know what some men never find out, that the woman who cannot discern when she is loved has never lived. It makes me laugh to think how successful I was in concealing it all; within a short time after our duet all of the friends of my dear one were referring to me as her "little sweetheart," or her "little beau," and she laughingly encouraged it. This did not entirely satisfy me; I wanted to be taken seriously. I had definitely made up my mind that I should never love another woman, and that if she deceived me I should do something desperate—the great difficulty was to think of something sufficiently desperate—and the heartless jade, how she led me on!

So I hurried home that afternoon, humming snatches of the violin part of the duet, my heart beating with pleasurable excitement over the fact that I was going to be near her, to have her attention placed directly upon me; that I was going to be of service to her, and in a way in which I could show myself to advantage—this last consideration has much to do with cheerful service.—The anticipation produced in me a sensation somewhat between bliss and fear. I rushed through the gate, took the three steps to the house at one bound, threw open the door, and was about to hang my cap on its accustomed peg of the hall rack when I noticed that that particular peg was occupied by a black derby hat. I stopped suddenly, and gazed at this hat as though I had never seen an object of its description. I was still looking at it in open-eyed wonder when my mother, coming out of the parlor into the hallway, called me, and said there was someone inside who wanted to see me. Feeling that I was being made a party to some kind of mystery I went in with her, and there I saw a man standing leaning with one elbow on the mantel, his back partly turned toward the door. As I entered he turned, and I saw a tall, handsome, well dressed gentleman of perhaps thirty-five; he advanced a step toward me with a smile on his face. I stopped and looked at him with the same feelings with which I had looked at the derby hat, except that they were greatly magnified. I looked at him from head to foot, but he was an absolute blank to me until my eyes rested on his slender, elegant, polished shoes; then it seemed that indistinct and partly obliterated films of memory began at first slowly then rapidly to unroll, forming a vague panorama of my childhood days in Georgia.

My mother broke the spell by calling me by name, and saying, "This is your father."

"Father, Father," that was the word which had been to me a source of doubt and perplexity ever since the interview with my mother on the subject. How often I had wondered about my father, who he was, what he was like, whether alive or dead, and above all, why she would not tell me about him. More than once I had been on the point of recalling to her the promise she had made me, but I instinctively felt that she was happier for not telling me and that I was happier for not being told; yet I had not the slightest idea what the real truth was. And here he stood before me, just the kind of looking father I had wishfully pictured him to be; but I made no advance toward him; I stood there feeling embarrassed and foolish, not knowing what to say or do. I am not sure but that he felt pretty much the same. My mother stood at my side with one hand on my shoulder almost pushing me forward, but I did not move. I can well remember the look of disappointment, even pain, on her face and I can now understand that she could expect nothing else but that at the name "father" I should throw myself into his arms. But I could not rise to this dramatic or, better, melodramatic climax. Somehow I could not arouse any considerable feeling of need for a father. He broke the awkward tableau by saying, "Well, boy, aren't you glad to see me?" He evidently meant the words kindly enough, but I don't know what he could have said that would have had a worse effect; however, my good breeding came to my rescue, and I answered, "Yes, sir," and went to him and offered him my hand. He took my hand into one of his, and, with the other, stroked my head saying that I had grown into a fine youngster. He asked me how old I was; which, of course, he must have done merely to say something more, or perhaps he did so as a test of my intelligence. I replied, "Twelve, sir." He then made the trite observation about the flight of time, and we lapsed into another awkward pause.

My mother was all in smiles; I believe that was one of the happiest moments of her life. Either to put me more at ease or to show me off, she asked me to play something for my father. There is only one thing in the world that can make music, at all times and under all circumstances, up to its general standard, that is a hand-organ, or one of its variations. I went to the piano and played something in a listless, half-hearted way. I simply was not in the mood. I was wondering, while playing, when my mother would dismiss me and let me go; but my father was so enthusiastic in his praise that he touched my vanity—which was great—and more than that; he displayed that sincere appreciation which always arouses an artist to his best effort, and, too, in an unexplainable manner, makes him feel like shedding tears. I showed my gratitude by playing for him a Chopin waltz with all the feeling that was in me. When I had finished my mother's eyes were glistening with tears; my father stepped across the room, seized me in his arms, and squeezed me to his breast. I am certain that for that moment he was proud to be my father. He sat and held me standing between his knees while he talked to my mother. I, in the meantime, examined him with more curiosity, perhaps, than politeness. I interrupted the conversation by asking, "Mother, is he going to stay with us now?" I found it impossible to frame the word "father" it was too new to me; so I asked the question through my mother. Without waiting for her to speak, my father answered, "I've got to go back to New York this afternoon, but I'm coming to see you again." I turned abruptly and went over to my mother, and almost in a whisper reminded her that I had an appointment which I should not miss; to my pleasant surprise she said that she would give me something to eat at once so that I might go. She went out of the room, and I began to gather from off the piano the music I needed. When I had finished, my father, who had been watching me, asked, "Are you going?" I replied, "Yes, sir, I've got to go to practice for a concert." He spoke some words of advice to me about being a good boy and taking care of my mother when I grew up, and added that he was going to send me something nice from New York. My mother called, and I said good-by to him, and went out. I saw him only once after that.

I quickly swallowed down what my mother had put on the table for me, seized my cap and music, and hurried off to my teacher's house. On the way I could think of nothing but this new father, where he came from, where he had been, why he was here, and why he would not stay. In my mind I ran over the whole list of fathers I had become acquainted with in my reading, but I could not classify him. The thought did not cross my mind that he was different from me, and even if it had the mystery would not thereby have been explained; for notwithstanding my changed relations with most of my schoolmates, I had only a faint knowledge of prejudice and no idea at all how it ramified and affected the entire social organism. I felt, however, that there was something about the whole affair which had to be hid.

When I arrived I found that she of the brown eyes had been rehearsing with my teacher, and was on the point of leaving. My teacher with some expressions of surprise asked why I was late, and I stammered out the first deliberate lie of which I have any recollection. I told him that when I reached home from school I found my mother quite sick, and that I had stayed with her a while before coming. Then unnecessarily and gratuitously, to give my words force of conviction, I suppose, I added, "I don't think she'll be with us very long." In speaking these words I must have been comical; for I noticed that my teacher, instead of showing signs of anxiety or sorrow, half hid a smile. But how little did I know that in that lie I was speaking a prophecy.

She of the brown eyes unpacked her violin, and we went through the duet several times. I was soon lost to all other thoughts in the delights of music and love. I say delights of love without reservation; for at no time of life is love so pure, so delicious, so poetic, so romantic, as it is in boyhood. A great deal has been said about the heart of a girl when she stands "where the brook and river meet," but what she feels is negative; more interesting is the heart of a boy when just at the budding dawn of manhood he stands looking wide-eyed into the long vistas opening before him; when he first becomes conscious of the awakening and quickening of strange desires and unknown powers; when what he sees and feels is still shadowy and mystical enough to be intangible, and, so, more beautiful; when his imagination is unsullied, and his faith new and whole—then it is that love wears a halo—the man who has not loved before he was fourteen has missed a fore-taste of Elysium.

When I reached home it was quite dark, and I found my mother without a light, sitting rocking in a chair as she so often used to do in my childhood days, looking into the fire and singing softly to herself. I nestled close to her, and with her arms around me she haltingly told me who my father was,—a great man, a fine gentleman,—he loved me and loved her very much; he was going to make a great man of me. All she said was so limited by reserve and so colored by her feelings that it was but half truth; and so, I did not yet fully understand.

CHAPTER III

Perhaps I ought not pass on this narrative without mentioning that the duet was a great success; so great that we were obliged to respond with two encores. It seemed to me that life could hold no greater joy than it contained when I took her hand and we stepped down to the front of the stage bowing to our enthusiastic audience. When we reached the little dressing-room, where the other performers were applauding as wildly as the audience, she impulsively threw both her arms around me, and kissed me, while I struggled to get away.

One day a couple of weeks after my father had been to see us, a wagon drove up to our cottage loaded with a big box. I was about to tell the man on the wagon that they had made a mistake, when my mother, acting darkly wise, told them to bring their load in; she had them to unpack the box, and quickly there was evolved from the boards, paper and other packing material, a beautiful, brand new, upright piano. Then she informed me that it was a present to me from my father. I at once sat down and ran my fingers over the keys; the full, mellow tone of the instrument was ravishing. I thought, almost remorsefully, of how I had left my father; but, even so, there momentarily crossed my mind a feeling of disappointment that the piano was not a grand. The new instrument greatly increased the pleasure of my hours of study and practice at home.

Shortly after this I was made a member of the boys' choir, it being found that I possessed a clear, strong soprano voice. I enjoyed the singing very much. About a year later I began the study of the pipe organ and the theory of music; and before I finished the grammar school I had written out several simple preludes for organ which won the admiration of my teacher, and which he did me the honor to play at services.

The older I grew the more thought I gave to the question of my and my mother's position, and what was our exact relation to the world in general. My idea of the whole matter was rather hazy. My study of United States history had been confined to those periods which were designated in my book as "Discovery," "Colonial," "Revolutionary," and "Constitutional." I now began to study about the Civil War, but the story was told in such a condensed and skipping style that I gained from it very little real information. It is a marvel how children ever learn any history out of books of that sort. And, too, I began now to read the newspapers; I often saw articles which aroused my curiosity, but did not enlighten me. But, one day, I drew from the circulating library a book that cleared the whole mystery, a book that I read with the same feverish intensity with which I had read the old Bible stories, a book that gave me my first perspective of the life I was entering; that book was "Uncle Tom's Cabin."

This work of Harriet Beecher Stowe has been the object of much unfavorable criticism. It has been assailed, not only as fiction of the most imaginative sort, but as being a direct misrepresentation. Several successful attempts have lately been made to displace the book from northern school libraries. Its critics would brush it aside with the remark that there never was a Negro as good as Uncle Tom, nor a slave-holder as bad as Lagree. For my part, I was never an admirer of Uncle Tom, nor of his type of goodness; but I believe that there were lots of old Negroes as foolishly good as he; the proof of which is that they knowingly stayed and worked the plantations that furnished sinews for the army which was fighting to keep them enslaved. But, in these later years, several cases have come to my personal knowledge in which old Negroes have died and left what was a considerable fortune to the descendants of their former masters. I do not think it takes any great stretch of the imagination to believe there was a fairly large class of slave holders typified in Lagree. And we must also remember that the author depicted a number of worthless if not vicious Negroes, and a slave holder who was as much of a Christian and a gentleman as it was possible for one in his position to be; that she pictured the happy, singing, shuffling darkey as well as the mother waiting for her child sold "down river."

I do not think it is claiming too much to say that "Uncle Tom's Cabin" was a fair and truthful panorama of slavery; however that may be, it opened my eyes as to who and what I was and what my country considered me; in fact, it gave me my bearing. But there was no shock; I took the whole revelation in a kind of stoical way. One of the greatest benefits I derived from reading the book was that I could afterwards talk frankly with my mother on all the questions which had been vaguely troubling my mind. As a result, she was entirely freed from reserve, and often herself brought up the subject, talking of things directly touching her life and mine and of things which had come down to her through the "old folks." What she told me interested and even fascinated me; and, what may seem strange, kindled in me a strong desire to see the South. She spoke to me quite frankly about herself, my father and myself; she, the sewing girl of my father's mother; he, an impetuous young man home from college; I, the child of this unsanctioned love. She told me even the principal reason for our coming North. My father was about to be married to a young lady of another great Southern family. She did not neglect to add that another reason for our being in Connecticut was that he intended to give me an education, and make a man of me. In none of her talks did she ever utter one word of complaint against my father. She always endeavored to impress upon me how good he had been and still was, and that he was all to us that custom and the law would allow. She loved him; more, she worshiped him, and she died firmly believing that he loved her more than any other woman in the world. Perhaps she was right. Who knows?

All of these newly awakened ideas and thoughts took the form of a definite aspiration on the day I graduated from the grammar school. And what a day that was! The girls in white dresses with fresh ribbons in their hair; the boys in new suits and creaky shoes; the great crowd of parents and friends, the flowers, the prizes and congratulations, made the day seem to me one of the greatest importance. I was on the programme, and played piano solo which was received by the audience with that amount of applause which I had come to look upon as being only the just due to my talent.

But the real enthusiasm was aroused by "Shiny." He was the principal speaker of the and well did he measure up to the honor. He made a striking picture, that thin little black boy standing on the platform, dressed in clothes that did not fit him any too well, his eyes burning with excitement, his shrill, musical voice vibrating in tones of appealing defiance, and his black face alight with such great intelligence and earnestness as to be positively handsome. What were his thoughts when he stepped forward and looked into that crowd of faces, all white with the exception of a score or so that were lost to view. I do not know, but I fancy he felt his loneliness. I think there must have rushed over him a feeling akin to that of a gladiator tossed into the arena and bade to fight for his life. I think that solitary little black figure standing there felt that for the particular time and place he bore the weight and responsibility of his race; that for him to fail meant general defeat; but he won, and nobly. His oration was Wendell Phillips' "Toussant L'Ouverture," a speech which may now be classed as rhetorical, even, perhaps, bombastic; but as the words fell from "Shiny's" lips their effect was magical. How so young an orator could stir so great enthusiasm was to be wondered at. When in the famous peroration, his voice trembling with suppressed emotion rose higher and higher and then rested on the name Toussant L'Ouverture, it was like touching an electric button which loosed the pent-up feelings of his listeners. They actually rose to him.

I have since known of colored men who have been chosen as class orators in our leading universities, of others who have played on the Varsity foot-hall and baseball teams, of colored speakers who have addressed great white audiences. In each of these instances I believe the men were stirred by the same emotions which actuated "Shiny" on the day of his graduation; and, too, in each ease where the efforts have reached any high standard of excellence they have been followed by the same phenomenon of enthusiasm. I think the explanation of the latter lies in what is a basic, though often dormant, principle of the Anglo-Saxon heart, love of fair play. "Shiny," it is true, was what is so common in his race, a natural orator; but I doubt that any white boy of equal talent could have wrought the same effect. The sight of that boy gallantly waging with puny, black arms, so unequal a battle, touched the deep springs in the hearts of his audience, and they were swept by a wave of sympathy and admiration.

But the effect upon me of "Shiny's" speech was double; I not only shared the enthusiasm of his audience, but he imparted to me some of his own enthusiasm. I felt leap within me pride that I was colored; and I began to form wild dreams of bringing glory and honor to the Negro race. For days I could talk of nothing else with my mother except my ambitions to be a great man, a great colored man, to reflect credit on the race, and gain fame for myself. It was not until years after that I formulated a definite and feasible plan for realizing my dreams.

I entered the high school with my class, and still continued my study of the piano, the pipe organ and the theory of music. I had to drop out of the boys' choir on account of a changing voice; this I regretted very much. As I grew older my love for reading grew stronger. I read with studious interest everything I could find relating to colored men who had gained prominence. My heroes had been King David, then Robert the Bruce; now Frederick Douglass was enshrined in the place of honor. When I learned that Alexander Dumas was a colored man, I re-read "Monte Cristo" and "The Three Guardsmen" with magnified pleasure. I lived between my music and books, on the whole a rather unwholesome life for a boy to lead. I dwelt in a world of imagination, of dreams and air castles,—the kind of atmosphere that sometimes nourishes a genius, more often men unfitted for the practical struggles of life. I never played a game of ball, never went fishing or learned to swim; in fact, the only outdoor exercise in which I took any interest was skating. Nevertheless, though slender, I grew well-formed and in perfect health. After I entered the high school I began to notice the change in my mother's health, which I suppose had been going on for some years. She began to complain a little and to cough a great deal; she tried several remedies, and finally went to see a doctor; but though she was failing in health she kept her spirits up. She still did a great deal of sewing, and in the busy seasons hired two women to help her. The purpose she had formed of having me go through college without financial worries kept her at work when she was not fit for it. I was so fortunate as to be able to organize a class of eight or ten beginners on the piano, and so start a separate little fund of my own. As the time for my graduation from the high school grew nearer, the plans for my college career became the chief subject of our talks. I sent for catalogues of all the prominent schools in the East, and eagerly gathered all the information I could concerning them from different sources. My mother told me that my father wanted me to go to Harvard or Yale; she herself had a half desire for me to go to Atlanta University, and even had me write for a catalogue of that school. There were two reasons, however, that inclined her to my father's choice: the first, that at Harvard or Yale I should be near her; the second, that my father had promised to pay a part of my college education.

Both "Shiny" and "Red" came to my house quite often of evenings, and we used to talk over our plans and prospects for the future. Sometimes I would play for them, and they seemed to enjoy the music very much. My mother often prepared sundry southern dishes for them, which I am not sure but that they enjoyed more. "Shiny" had an uncle in Amherst, Mass., and he expected to live with him and work his way through Amherst College. "Red" declared that he had enough of school and that after he got his high school diploma he would get a position in a bank. It was his ambition to become a banker, and he felt sure of getting the opportunity through certain members of his family.

My mother barely had strength to attend the closing exercises of the high school when I graduated; and after that day she was seldom out of bed. She could no longer direct her work, and under the expense of medicines, doctors, and someone to look after her, our college fund began to diminish rapidly. Many of her customers and some of the neighbors were very kind, and frequently brought her nourishment of one kind or another. My mother realized what I did not, that she was mortally ill, and she had me write a long letter to my father. For some time past she had heard from him only at irregular intervals; we never received an answer. In those last days I often sat at her bedside and read to her until she fell asleep. Sometimes I would leave the parlor door open and play on the piano, just loud enough for the music to reach her. This she always enjoyed.

One night, near the end of July, after I had been watching beside her for some hours, I went into the parlor, and throwing myself into the big arm chair dozed off into a fitful sleep. I was suddenly aroused by one of the neighbors, who had come in to sit with her that night. She said, "Come to your mother at once." I hurried upstairs, and at the bedroom door met the woman who was acting as nurse. I noted with a dissolving heart the strange look of awe on her face. From my first glance at my mother, I discerned the light of death upon her countenance. I fell upon my knees beside the bed, and burying my face in the sheets sobbed convulsively. She died with the fingers of her left hand entwined in my hair.

I will not rake over this, one of the two sacred sorrows of my life; nor could I describe the feeling of unutterable loneliness that fell upon me. After the funeral I went to the house of my music teacher; he had kindly offered me the hospitality of his home for so long as I might need it. A few days later I moved my trunk, piano, my music and most of my books to his home; the rest of my books I divided between "Shiny" and "Red." Some of the household effects I gave to "Shiny's" mother and to two or three of the neighbors who had been kind to us during my mother's illness; the others I sold. After settling up my little estate I found that besides a good supply of clothes, a piano, some books and other trinkets, I had about two hundred dollars in cash.

The question of what I was to do now confronted me. My teacher suggested a concert tour; but both of us realized that I was too old to be exploited as an infant prodigy and too young and inexperienced to go before the public as a finished artist. He, however, insisted that the people of the town would generously patronize a benefit concert, so took up the matter, and made arrangements for such an entertainment. A more than sufficient number of people with musical and elocutionary talent volunteered their services to make a programme. Among these was my brown-eyed violinist. But our relations were not the same as they were when we had played our first duet together. A year or so after that time she had dealt me a crushing blow by getting married. I was partially avenged, however, by the fact that, though she was growing more beautiful, she was losing her ability to play the violin.

I was down on the programme for one number. My selection might have appeared at that particular time as a bit of affectation, but I considered it deeply appropriate; I played Beethoven's "Sonata Pathétique." When I sat down at the piano, and glanced into the faces of the several hundreds of people who were there solely on account of love or sympathy for me, emotions swelled in my heart which enabled me to play the "Pathétique" as I could never again play it. When the last tone died away the few who began to applaud were hushed by the silence of the others; and for once I played without receiving an encore.

The benefit yielded me a little more than two hundred dollars, thus raising my cash capital to about four hundred dollars. I still held to my determination of going to college; so it was now a question of trying to squeeze through a year at Harvard or going to Atlanta where the money I had would pay my actual expenses for at least two years. The peculiar fascination which the South held over my imagination and my limited capital decided me in favor of Atlanta University; so about the last of September I bade farewell to the friends and scenes of my boyhood, and boarded a train for the South.

CHAPTER IV

The farther I got below Washington the more disappointed I became in the appearance of the country. I peered through the car windows, looking in vain for the luxuriant semi-tropical scenery which I had pictured in my mind. I did not find the grass so green, nor the woods so beautiful, nor the flowers so plentiful, as they were in Connecticut. Instead, the red earth partly covered by tough, scrawny grass, the muddy straggling roads, the cottages of unpainted pine boards, and the clay daubed huts imparted a "burnt up" impression. Occasionally we ran through a little white and green village that was like an oasis in a desert.

When I reached Atlanta my steadily increasing disappointment was not lessened. I found it a big, dull, red town. This dull red color of that part of the South I was then seeing had much, I think, to do with the extreme depression of my spirits—no public squares, no fountains, dingy street-cars and, with the exception of three or four principal thoroughfares, unpaved streets. It was raining when I arrived and some of these unpaved streets were absolutely impassable. Wheels sank to the hubs in red mire, and I actually stood for an hour and watched four or five men work to save a mule, which had stepped into a deep sink, from drowning, or, rather, suffocating in the mud. The Atlanta of to-day is a new city.

On the train I had talked with one of the Pullman car porters, a bright young fellow who was himself a student, and told him that I was going to Atlanta to attend school. I had also asked him to tell me where I might stop for a day or two until the University opened. He said I might go with him to the place where he stopped during his "layovers" in Atlanta. I gladly accepted his offer, and went with him along one of those muddy streets until we came to a rather rickety looking frame house, which we entered. The proprietor of the house was a big, fat, greasy looking brown-skinned man. When I asked him if he could give me accommodation he wanted to know how long I would stay. I told him perhaps two days, not more than three. In reply he said, "Oh, dat's all right den," at the same time leading the way up a pair of creaky stairs. I followed him and the porter to a room, the door of which the proprietor opened while continuing, it seemed, his remark, "Oh, dat's all right den," by adding, "You kin sleep in dat cot in de corner der. Fifty cents please." The porter interrupted by saying, "You needn't collect from him now, he's got a trunk." This seemed to satisfy the man, and he went down leaving me and my porter friend in the room. I glanced around the apartment and saw that it contained a double bed and two cots, two wash-stands, three chairs, and a time-worn bureau with a looking-glass that would have made Adonis appear hideous. I looked at the cot in which I was to sleep and suspected, not without good reasons, that I should not be the first to use the sheets and pillow-case since they had last come from the wash. When I thought of the clean, tidy, comfortable surroundings in which I had been reared, a wave of homesickness swept over me that made me feel faint. Had it not been for the presence of my companion, and that I knew this much of his history,—that he was not yet quite twenty, just three years older than myself, and that he had been fighting his own way in the world, earning his own living and providing for his own education since he was fourteen, I should not have been able to stop the tears that were welling up in my eyes.

I asked him why it was that the proprietor of the house seemed unwilling to accommodate me for more than a couple of days. He informed me that the man ran a lodging house especially for Pullman porters, and as their stays in town were not longer than one or two nights it would interfere with his arrangements to have anyone stay longer. He went on to say, "You see this room is fixed up to accommodate four men at a time. Well, by keeping a sort of table of trips, in and out, of the men, and working them like checkers, he can accommodate fifteen or sixteen in each week, and generally avoid having an empty bed. You happen to catch a bed that would have been empty for a couple of nights." I asked him where he was going to sleep. He answered, "I sleep in that other cot to-night; to-morrow night I go out." He went on to tell me that the man who kept the house did not serve meals, and that if I was hungry we would go out and get something to eat.

We went into the street, and in passing the railroad station I hired a wagon to take my trunk to my lodging place. We passed along until, finally, we turned into a street that stretched away, up and down hill, for a mile or two; and here I caught my first sight of colored people in large numbers. I had seen little squads around the railroad stations on my way south; but here I saw a street crowded with them. They filled the shops and thronged the sidewalks and lined the curb. I asked my companion if all the colored people in Atlanta lived in this street. He said they did not, and assured me that the ones I saw were of the lower class. I felt relieved, in spite of the size of the lower class. The unkempt appearance, the shambling, slouching gait and loud talk and laughter of these people aroused in me a feeling of almost repulsion. Only one thing about them awoke a feeling of interest; that was their dialect. I had read some Negro dialect and had heard snatches of it on my journey down from Washington; but here I heard it in all of its fullness and freedom. I was particularly struck by the way in which it was punctuated by such exclamatory phrases as "Lawd a mussy!" "G'wan man!" "Bless ma soul!" "Look heah chile!" These people talked and laughed without restraint. In fact, they talked straight from their lungs, and laughed from the pits of their stomachs. And this hearty laughter was often justified by the droll humor of some remark. I paused long enough to hear one man say to another, "W'at's de mattah wid you an' yo' fr'en' Sam?" and the other came back like a flash, "Ma fr'en? He ma fr'en? Man! I'd go to his funeral jes de same as I'd go to a minstrel show." I have since learned that this ability to laugh heartily is, in part, the salvation of the American Negro; it does much to keep him from going the way of the Indian.

The business places of the street along which we were passing consisted chiefly of low bars, cheap dry-goods and notion stores, barber shops, and fish and bread restaurants. We, at length, turned down a pair of stairs that led to a basement, and I found myself in an eating-house somewhat better than those I had seen in passing; but that did not mean much for its excellence. The place was smoky, the tables were covered with oil-cloth, the floor covered with sawdust, and from the kitchen came a rancid odor of fish fried over several times, which almost nauseated me. I asked my companion if this were the place where we were to eat. He informed me that it was the best place in town where a colored man could get a meal. I then wanted to know why somebody didn't open a place where respectable colored people who had money could be accommodated. He answered, "It wouldn't pay; all the respectable colored people eat at home, and the few who travel generally have friends in the towns to which they go, who entertain them." He added, "Of course, you could go in any place in the city; they wouldn't know you from white."

I sat down with the porter at one of the tables, but was not hungry enough to eat with any relish what was put before me. The food was not badly cooked; but the iron knives and forks needed to be scrubbed, the plates and dishes and glasses needed to he washed and well dried. I minced over what I took on my plate while my companion ate. When we finished we paid the waiter twenty cents each and went out. We walked around until the lights of the city were lit. Then the porter said that he must get to bed and have some rest, he had not had six hours' sleep since he left Jersey City. I went back to our lodging-house with him.

When I awoke in the morning there were, besides my new found friend, two other men in the room, asleep in the double bed. I got up and dressed myself very quietly, so as not to awake anyone. I then drew from under the pillow my precious roll of greenbacks, took out a ten dollar bill, and very softly unlocking my trunk, put the remainder, about three hundred dollars, in the inside pocket of a coat near the bottom; glad of the opportunity to put it unobserved in a place of safety When I had carefully locked my trunk, I tiptoed toward the door with the intention of going out to look for a decent restaurant where I might get something fit to eat. As I was easing the door open, my porter friend said with a yawn, "Hello! You're going out?" I answered him, "Yes." "Oh!" he yawned again, "I guess I've had enough sleep; wait a minute, I'll go with you." For the instant his friendship bored and embarrassed me. I had visions of another meal in the greasy restaurant of the day before. He must have divined my thoughts; for he went on to say, "I know a woman across town who takes a few boarders; I think we can go over there and get a good breakfast." With a feeling of mingled fears and doubts regarding what the breakfast might be, I waited until he had dressed himself.

When I saw the neat appearance of the cottage we entered my fears vanished, and when I saw the woman who kept it my doubts followed the same course. Scrupulously clean, in a spotless white apron and colored head handkerchief, her round face beaming with motherly kindness, she was picturesquely beautiful. She impressed me as one broad expanse of happiness and good nature. In a few minutes she was addressing me as "chile" and "honey." She made me feel as though I should like to lay my head on her capacious bosom and go to sleep.

And the breakfast, simple as it was, I could not have had at any restaurant in Atlanta at any price. There was fried chicken, as it is fried only in the South, hominy boiled to the consistency where it could be eaten with a fork, and biscuits so light and flaky that a fellow with any appetite at all would have no difficulty in disposing of eight or ten. When I had finished I felt that I had experienced the realization of, at least, one of my dreams of Southern life.

During the meal we found out from our hostess, who had two boys in school, that Atlanta University opened on that very day. I had somehow mixed my dates. My friend the porter suggested that I go out to the University at once and offered to walk over and show me the way. We had to walk because, although the University was not more than twenty minutes distance from the center of the city, there were no street-cars running in that direction. My first sight of the school grounds made me feel that I was not far from home; here the red hills had been terraced and covered with green grass; clean gravel walks, well shaded, lead up to the buildings; indeed, it was a bit of New England transplanted. At the gate my companion said he would bid me good-by, because it was likely that he would not see me again before his car went out. He told me that he would make two more trips to Atlanta, and that he would come out and see me; that after his second trip he would leave the Pullman service for the winter and return to school in Nashville. We shook hands, I thanked him for all his kindness, and we said good-by.

I walked up to a group of students and made some inquiries. They directed me to the president's office in the main building. The president gave me a cordial welcome; it was more than cordial; he talked to me, not as the official head of a college, but as though he were adopting me into what was his large family, to personally look after my general welfare as well as my education. He seemed especially pleased with the fact that I had come to them all the way from the North. He told me that I could have come to the school as soon as I had reached the city, and that I had better move my trunk out at once. I gladly promised him that I would do so. He then called a boy and directed him to take me to the matron, and to show me around afterwards. I found the matron even more motherly than the president was fatherly. She had me to register, which was in effect to sign a pledge to abstain from the use of intoxicating beverages, tobacco, and profane language, while I was a student in the school. This act caused me no sacrifice; as, up to that time, I was free from either habit. The boy who was with me then showed me about the grounds. I was especially interested in the industrial building.

The sounding of a bell, he told me, was the signal for the students to gather in the general assembly hall, and he asked me if I would go. Of course would. There were between three and four hundred students and perhaps all of the teachers gathered in the room. I noticed that several of the latter were colored. The president gave a talk addressed principally to new comers but I scarcely heard what he said, I was so much occupied in looking at those around me. They were of all types and colors, the more intelligent types predominating. The colors ranged from jet black to pure white, with light hair and eyes. Among the girls especially there were many so fair that it was difficult to believe that they had Negro blood in them. And, too, I could not help but notice that many of the girls, particularly those of the delicate brown shades, with black eyes and wavy dark hair, were decidedly pretty. Among the boys, many of the blackest were fine specimens of young manhood, tall, straight, and muscular, with magnificent heads; these were the kind of boys who developed into the patriarchal "uncles" of the old slave régime.

When I left the University it was with the determination to get my trunk, and move out to the school before night. I walked back across the city with a light step and a light heart. I felt perfectly satisfied with life for the first time since my mother's death. In passing the railroad station I hired a wagon and rode with the driver as far as my stopping place. I settled with my landlord and went upstairs to put away several articles I had left out. As soon as I opened my trunk a dart of suspicion shot through my heart; the arrangement of things did not look familiar. I began to dig down excitedly to the bottom till I reached the coat in which I had concealed my treasure. My money was gone! Every single bill of it. I knew it was useless to do so, but I searched through every other coat, every pair of trousers, every vest, and even into each pair of socks. When I had finished my fruitless search I sat down dazed and heartsick. I called the landlord up, and informed him of my loss; he comforted me by saying that I ought to have better sense than to keep money in a trunk, and that he was not responsible for his lodgers' personal effects. His cooling words brought me enough to my senses to cause me to look and see if anything else was missing. Several small articles were gone, among them a black and gray necktie of odd design upon which my heart was set; almost as much as the loss of my money, I felt the loss of my tie.

After thinking for awhile as best I could, I wisely decided to go at once back to the University and lay my troubles before the president. I rushed breathlessly back to the school. As I neared the grounds the thought came across me, would not my story sound fishy? Would it not place me in the position of an impostor or beggar? What right had I to worry these busy people with the results of my carelessness? If the money could not be recovered, and I doubted that it could, what good would it do to tell them about it. The shame and embarrassment which the whole situation gave me caused me to stop at the gate. I paused, undecided, for a moment; then turned and slowly retraced my steps, and so changed the whole course of my life.

If the reader has never been in a strange city without money or friends, it is useless to try to describe what my feelings were; he could not understand. If he has been, it is equally useless, for he understands more than words could convey. When I reached my lodgings I found in the room one of the porters who had slept there the night before. When he heard what misfortune had befallen me he offered many words of sympathy and advice. He asked me how much money I had left, I told him that I had ten or twelve dollars in my pocket. He said, "That won't last you very long here, and you will hardly be able to find anything to do in Atlanta. I'll tell you what you do, go down to Jacksonville and you won't have any trouble to get a job in one of the big hotels there, or in St. Augustine." I thanked him, but intimated my doubts of being able to get to Jacksonville on the money I had. He reassured me by saying, "Oh, that's all right. You express your trunk on through, and I'll take you down in my closet." I thanked him again, not knowing then, what it was to travel in a Pullman porter's closet. He put me under a deeper debt of gratitude by lending me fifteen dollars, which he said I could pay back after I had secured work. His generosity brought tears to my eyes, and I concluded that, after all, there were some kind hearts in the world.

I now forgot my troubles in the hurry and excitement of getting my trunk off in time to catch the train, which went out at seven o'clock. I even forgot that I hadn't eaten anything since morning. We got a wagon—the porter went with me—and took my trunk to the express office. My new friend then told me to come to the station at about a quarter of seven, and walk straight to the car where I should see him standing, and not to lose my nerve. I found my rôle not so difficult to play as I thought it would he, because the train did not leave from the central station, but from a smaller one, where there were no gates and guards to pass. I followed directions, and the porter took me on his car, and locked me in his closet. In a few minutes the train pulled out for Jacksonville.

I may live to be a hundred years old. but I shall never forget the agonies I suffered that night. I spent twelve hours doubled up in the porter's basket for soiled linen, not being able to straighten up on account of the shelves for clean linen just over my head.. The air was hot and suffocating and the smell of damp towels and used linen was sickening. At each lurch of the car over the none too smooth track, I was bumped and bruised against the narrow walls of my narrow compartment. I became acutely conscious of the fact that I had not eaten for hours. Then nausea took possession of me, and at one time I had grave doubts about reaching my destination alive. If I had the trip to make again, I should prefer to walk.

CHAPTER V

The next morning I got out of the car at Jacksonville with a stiff and aching body. I determined to ask no more porters, not even my benefactor, about stopping places; so I found myself on the street not knowing where to go. I walked along listlessly until I met a colored man who had the appearance of a preacher. I asked him if he could direct me to a respectable boarding-house for colored people. He said that if I walked along with him in the direction he was going he would show me such a place. I turned and walked at his side. He proved to he a minister, and asked me a great many direct questions about myself. I answered as many as I saw fit to answer; the others I evaded or ignored. At length. we stopped in front of a frame house, and my guide informed me that it was the place. A woman was standing in the doorway, and he called to her saying that he had brought her a new boarder. I thanked him for his trouble, and after he had urged upon me to attend his church while I was in the city, he went on his way.

I went in and found the house neat and not uncomfortable. The parlor was furnished with cane-bottomed chairs, each of which was adorned with a white crocheted tidy. The mantel over the fireplace had a white crocheted cover; a marble-topped center table held a lamp, a photograph album and several trinkets, each of which was set upon a white crocheted mat. There was a cottage organ in a corner of the room, and I noted that the lamp-racks upon it were covered with white crocheted mats. There was a matting on the floor, but a white crocheted carpet would not have been out of keeping. I made arrangements with the landlady for my hoard and lodging; the amount was, I think, three dollars and a half a week. She was a rather fine looking, stout, brown-skinned woman of about forty years of age. Her husband was a light colored Cuban, a man about one half her size, and one whose age could not be guessed from his appearance. He was small in ize, but a handsome black mustache and typical Spanish eyes redeemed him from insignificance.

I was in time for breakfast, and at the table I had the opportunity to see my fellow-boarders. There were eight or ten of them. Two, as I afterwards learned, were colored Americans. All of them were cigar makers and worked in one of the large factories—cigar making is the one trade in which the color-line is not drawn. The conversation was carried on entirely in Spanish, and my ignorance of the language subjected me more to alarm than embarrassment. I had never heard such uproarious conversation; everybody talked at once, loud exclamations, rolling "carambas," menacing gesticulations with knives, forks, and spoons. I looked every moment for the clash of blows. One man was emphasizing his remarks by flourishing a cup in his hand, seemingly forgetful of the fact that it was nearly full of hot coffee. He ended by emptying it over what was, relatively, the only quiet man at the table excepting myself, bringing from him a volley of language which made the others appear dumb by comparison. I soon learned that in all of this clatter of voices and table utensils they were discussing purely ordinary affairs and arguing about mere trifles, and that not the least ill-feeling was aroused. It was not long before I enjoyed the spirited chatter and badinage at the table as much as I did my meals,—and the meals were not bad.

I spent the afternoon in looking around the town. The streets were sandy, but were well shaded by fine oak trees, and far preferable to the clay roads of Atlanta. One or two public squares with green grass and trees gave the city a touch of freshness. That night after supper I spoke to my landlady and her husband about my intentions. They told me that the big winter hotels would not open within two months. It can easily be imagined what effect this news had on me. I spoke to them frankly about my financial condition and related the main fact of my misfortune in Atlanta. I modestly mentioned my ability to teach music and asked if there was any likelihood of my being able to get some scholars. My landlady suggested that I speak to the preacher who had shown me her house; she felt sure that through his influence I should be able to get up a class in piano. She added, however, that the colored people were poor, and that the general price for music lessons was only twenty-five cents. I noticed that the thought of my teaching white pupils did not even remotely enter her mind. None of this information made my prospects look much brighter .

The husband, who up to this time had allowed the woman to do most of the talking, gave me the first bit of tangible hope; he said that he could get me a job as a "stripper" in the factory where he worked, and that if I succeeded in getting some music pupils I could teach a couple of them every night, and so make a living until something better turned up. He went on to say that it would not be a bad thing for me to stay at the factory and learn my trade as a cigar maker, and impressed on me that, for a young man knocking about the country, a trade was a handy thing to have. I determined to accept his offer and thanked him heartily. In fact, I became enthusiastic, not only because I saw a way out of my financial troubles, but also because I was eager and curious over the new experience I was about to enter. I Wanted to know all about the cigar making business. This narrowed the conversation down to the husband and myself, so the wife went in and left us talking.

He was what is called a regaliá workman, and earned from thirty-five to forty dollars a week. He generally worked a sixty dollar job; that is, he made cigars for which he was paid at the rate of sixty dollars per thousand. It was impossible for him to make a thousand in a week because he had to work very carefully and slowly. Each cigar was made entirely by hand. Each piece of filler and each wrapper had to be selected with care. He was able to make a bundle of one hundred cigars in a day, not one of which could be told from the others by any difference in size or shape, or even by any appreciable difference in weight. This was the acme of artistic skill in cigar making. Workmen of this class were rare, never more than three or four of them in one factory, and it was never necessary for them to remain out of work. There were men who made two, three, and four hundred cigars of the cheaper grades in a day; they had to be very fast in order to make decent week's wages. Cigar making was a rather independent trade; the men went to work when they pleased and knocked off when they felt like doing so. As a class the workmen were careless and improvident; some very rapid makers would not work more than three or four days out of the week, and there were others who never showed up at the factory on Mondays. "Strippers" were the boys who pulled the long stems from the tobacco leaves. After they had served at that work for a certain time they were given tables as apprentices.

All of this was interesting to me; and we drifted along in conversation until my companion struck the subject nearest his heart, the independence of Cuba. He was an exile from the island, and a prominent member of the Jacksonville Junta. Every week sums of money were collected from juntas all over the country. This money went to buy arms and ammunition for the insurgents. As the man sat there nervously smoking his long, "green" cigar, and telling me of the Gomezes, both the white one and the black one, of Macco and Bandera, he grew positively eloquent. He also showed that he was a man of considerable education and reading. He spoke English excellently, and frequently surprised me by using words one would hardly expect from a foreigner. The first one of this class of words he employed almost shocked me, and I never forgot it, 'twas "ramify." We sat on the piazza until after ten o'clock. When e arose to go in to bed it was with the understanding that I should start in the factory on the next day.

I began work the next morning seated at a barrel with another boy, who showed me how to strip the stems from the leaves, to smooth out each half leaf, and to put the "rights" together in one pile, and the "lefts" together in another pile on the edge of the barrel. My fingers, strong and sensitive from their long training, were well adapted to this kind of work; and within two weeks I was accounted the fastest "stripper" in the factory. At first the heavy odor of the tobacco almost sickened me; but when I became accustomed to it I liked the smell. I was now earning four dollars a week, and was soon able to pick up a couple more by teaching a few scholars at night, whom I had secured through the good offices of the preacher I had met on my first morning in Jacksonville.

At the end of about three months, through my skill as a "stripper" and the influence of my landlord, I was advanced to a table, and began to learn my trade; in fact, more than my trade; for I learned not only to make cigars, but also to smoke, to swear, and to speak Spanish. I discovered that I had a talent for languages as well as for music. The rapidity and ease with which I acquired Spanish astonished my associates. In a short time I was able not only to understand most of what was said at the table during meals, but to join in the conversation. I bought a method for learning the Spanish language, and with the aid of my landlord as a teacher, by constant practice with my fellow workmen, and by regularly reading the Cuban newspapers, and finally some books of standard Spanish literature which were at the house, I was able in less than a year to speak like a native. In fact, it was my pride that I spoke better Spanish than many of the Cuban workmen at the factory.

After I had been in the factory a little over a year, I was repaid for all the effort I had put forth to learn Spanish by being selected as "reader." The "reader" is quite an institution in all cigar factories which employ Spanish-speaking workmen. He sits in the center of the large room in which the cigar makers work and reads to them for a certain number of hours each day all the important news from the papers and whatever else he may consider would be interesting. He often selects an exciting novel, and reads it in daily installments. He must, of course, have a good voice, but he must also have a reputation among the men for intelligence, for being well posted and having in his head a stock of varied information. He is generally the final authority on all arguments which arise; and, in a cigar factory, these arguments are many and frequent, ranging from discussions on the respective and relative merits of rival baseball clubs to the duration of the sun's light and energy—cigar-making is a trade in which talk does not interfere with work. My position as "reader" not only released me from the rather monotonous work of rolling cigars, and gave me something more in accord with my tastes, but also added considerably to my income. I was now earning about twenty-five dollars a week, and was able to give up my peripatetic method of giving music lessons. I hired a piano and taught only those who could arrange to take their lessons where I lived. I finally gave up teaching entirely; as what I made scarcely paid for my time and trouble. I kept the piano, however, in order to keep up my own studies, and occasionally I played at some church concert or other charitable entertainment.

Through my music teaching and my not absolutely irregular attendance at church I became acquainted with the best class of colored people in Jacksonville. This was really my entrance into the race. It was my initiation into what I have termed the freemasonry of the race. I had formulated a theory of what it was to be colored, now I was getting the practice. The novelty of my position caused me to observe and consider things which, I think, entirely escaped the young men I associated with; or, at least, were so commonplace to them as not to attract their attention. And of many of the impressions which came to me then I have realized the full import only within the past few years, since I have had a broader knowledge of men and history, and a fuller comprehension of the tremendous struggle which is going on between the races in the South.

It is a struggle; for though the black man fights passively he nevertheless fights; and his passive resistance is more effective at present than active resistance could possibly be. He bears the fury of the storm as does the willow tree.

It is a struggle; for though the white man of the South may be too proud to admit it, he is, nevertheless, using in the contest his best energies; he is devoting to it the greater part of his thought and much of his endeavor. The South to-day stands panting and almost breathless from its exertions.

And how the scene of the struggle has shifted! The battle was first waged over the right of the Negro to be classed as a human being with a soul; later, as to whether he had sufficient intellect to master even the rudiments of learning; and to-day it is being fought out over his social recognition.

I said somewhere in the early part of this narrative that because the colored man looked at everything through the prism of his relationship to society as a colored man, and because most of his mental efforts ran through the narrow channel bounded by his rights and his wrongs, it was to be wondered at that he has progressed so broadly as he has. The same thing may be said of the white man of the South; most of his mental efforts run through one narrow channel; his life as a man and a citizen, many of his financial activities and all of his political activities are impassably limited by the ever present "Negro question." I am sure it would be safe to wager that no group of Southern white men could get together and talk for sixty minutes without bringing up the "race question." If a Northern white man happened to be in the group the time could be safely cut to thirty minutes. In this respect I consider the condition of the whites more to be deplored than that of the blacks. Here, a truly great people, a people that produced a majority of the great historic Americans from Washington to Lincoln now forced to use up its energies in a conflict as lamentable as it is violent.

I shall give the observations I made in Jacksonville as seen through the light of after years; and they apply generally to every Southern community. The colored people may he said to be roughly divided into three classes, not so much in respect to themselves as in respect to their relations with the whites. There are those constituting what might be called the desperate class,—the men who work in the lumber and turpentine camps, the ex-convicts, the bar-room loafers are all in this class. These men conform to the requirements of civilization much as a trained lion with low muttered growls goes through his stunts under the crack of the trainer's whip. They cherish a sullen hatred for all white men, and they value life as cheap. I have heard more than one of them say, "I'll go to hell for the first white man that bothers me." Many who have expressed that sentiment have kept their word; and it is that fact which gives such prominence to this class; for in numbers it is but a small proportion of the colored people, but it often dominates public opinion concerning the whole race. Happily, this class represents the black people of the South far below their normal physical and moral condition, but in its increase lies the possibility of grave dangers. I am sure there is no more urgent work before the white South, not only for its present happiness, but its future safety, than the decreasing of this class of blacks. And it is not at all a hopeless class; for these men are but the creatures of conditions, as much so as the slum and criminal elements of all the great cities of the world are creatures of conditions. Decreasing their number by shooting and burning them off will not be successful; for these men are truly desperate, and thoughts of death, however terrible, have little effect in deterring them from acts the result of hatred or degeneracy. This class of blacks hate everything covered by a white skin, and in return they are loathed by the whites. The whites regard them just about as a man would a vicious mule, a thing to be worked, driven and beaten, and killed for kicking.

The second class, as regards the relation between blacks and whites, comprises the servants, the washer-women, the waiters, the cooks, the coachmen, and all who are connected with the whites by domestic service. These may be generally characterized as simple, kindhearted and faithful; not over fine in their moral deductions, but intensely religious, and relatively,—such matters can be judged only relatively,—about as honest and wholesome in their lives as any other grade of society. Any white person is "good" who treats them kindly, and they love them for that kindness. In return, the white people with whom they have to do regard them with indulgent affection. They come into close daily contact with the whites, and may be called the connecting link between whites and blacks; in fact, it is through them that the whites know the rest of their colored neighbors. Between this class of the blacks and the whites there is little or no friction.

The third class is composed of the independent workmen and tradesmen, and of the well-to-do and educated colored people; and, strange to say, for a directly opposite reason they are as far removed from the whites as the members of the first class I mentioned. These people live in a little world of their own; in fact, I concluded that if a colored man wanted to separate himself from his white neighbors he had but to acquire some money, education and culture, and to live in accordance. For example, the proudest and fairest lady in the South could with propriety—and it is what she would most likely do—go to the cabin of Aunt Mary her cook, if Aunt Mary were sick, and minister to comfort with her own hands; but if Mary's daughter, Eliza, a girl who used to run around my lady's kitchen, but who has received an education and married a prosperous young colored man, were at death's door, my lady would no more think of crossing the threshold of Eliza's cottage than she would of going into a bar-room for a drink.

I was walking down the street one day with a young man who was born in Jacksonville, but had been away to prepare himself for a professional life. We passed a young white man, and my companion said to me, "You see that young man? We grew up together, we have played, hunted, and fished together, we have even eaten and slept together, and now since I have come back home he barely speaks to me." The fact that the whites of the South despise and ill-treat the desperate class of blacks is not only explainable according to the ancient laws of human nature, but it is not nearly so serious or important as the fact that as the progressive colored people advance they constantly widen the gulf between themselves and their white neighbors. I think that the white people somehow feel that colored people who have education and money, who wear good clothes and live in comfortable houses, are "putting on airs," that they do these things for the sole purpose of "spiting the white folks," or are, at best, going through a sort of monkey-like imitation. Of course, such feelings can only cause irritation or breed disgust. It seems that the whites have not yet been able to realize and understand that these people in striving to better their physical and social surroundings in accordance with their financial and intellectual progress are simply obeying an impulse which is common to human nature the world over. I am in grave doubt as to whether the greater part of the friction in the South is caused by the whites having a natural antipathy to Negroes as a race, or an acquired antipathy to Negroes in certain relations to themselves. However that may be, there is to my mind no more pathetic side of this many sided question than the isolated position into which are forced the very colored people who most need and who could best appreciate sympathetic coöperation; and their position grows tragic when the effort is made to couple them, whether or no, with the Negroes of the first class I mentioned.

This latter class of colored people are well disposed towards the whites, and always willing to meet them more than half way. They, however, feel keenly any injustice or gross discrimination, and generally show their resentment. The effort is sometimes made to convey the impression that the better class of colored people fight against riding in "jim crow" cars because they want to ride with white people or object to being with humbler members of their own race. The truth is they object to the humiliation of being forced to ride in a particular car, aside from the fact that that car is distinctly inferior, and that they are required to pay full first-class fare. To say that the whites are forced to ride in the superior car is less than a joke. And, too, odd as it may sound, refined colored people get no more pleasure out of riding with offensive Negroes than anybody else would get.

I can realize more fully than I could years ago that the position of the advanced element of the colored race is often very trying. They are the ones among the blacks who carry the entire weight of the race question; it worries the others very little, and I believe the only thing which at times sustains them is that they know that they are in the right. On the other hand, this class of colored people get a good deal of pleasure out of life; their existence is far from being one long groan about their condition. Out of a chaos of ignorance and poverty they have evolved a social life of which they need not be ashamed. In cities where the professional and well-to-do class is large, they have formed society,—society as discriminating as the actual conditions will allow it to be; I should say, perhaps, society possessing discriminating tendencies which become rules as fast as actual conditions allow. This statement will, I know, sound preposterous, even ridiculous, to some persons; but as this class of colored people is the least known of the race it is not surprising. These social circles are connected throughout the country, and a person in good standing in one city is readily accepted in another. One who is on the outside will often find it a difficult matter to get in. I know of one case personally in which money to the extent of thirty or forty thousand dollars and a fine house, not backed up by a good reputation, after several years of repeated effort, failed to gain entry for the possessor. These people have their dances and dinners and card parties, their musicals and their literary societies. The women attend social affairs dressed in good taste, and the men in evening dress-suits which they own; and the reader will make a mistake to confound these entertainments with the "Bellman's Balls" and "Whitewashers' Picnics" and "Lime Kiln Clubs" with which the humorous press of the country illustrates "Cullud Sassiety."

Jacksonville, when I was there, was a small town, and the number of educated and well-to-do colored people was few; so this society phase of life did not equal what I have since seen in Boston, Washington, Richmond, and Nashville; and it is upon what I have more recently seen in these cities that I have made the observations just above. However, there were many comfortable and pleasant homes in Jacksonville to which I was often invited. I belonged to the literary society—at which we generally discussed the race question—and attended all of the church festivals and other charitable entertainments. In this way I passed three years which were not at all the least enjoyable of my life. In fact, my joy took such an exuberant turn that I fell in love with a young school teacher and began to have dreams of matrimonial bliss; but another turn in the course of my life brought these dreams to an end.

I do not wish to mislead my readers into thinking that I led a life in Jacksonville which would make copy as the hero of a Sunday School library book. I was a hale fellow well met with all of the workmen at the factory, most of whom knew little and cared less about social distinctions. From their example I learned to be careless about money; and for that reason I constantly postponed and finally abandoned returning to Atlanta University. It seemed impossible for me to save as much as two hundred dollars. Several of the men at the factory were my intimate friends, and I frequently joined them in their pleasures. During the summer months we went almost every Monday on an excursion to a seaside resort called Pablo Beach. These excursions were always crowded. There was a dancing pavilion, a great deal of drinking and generally a fight or two to add to the excitement. I also contracted the cigar-maker's habit of riding around in a hack on Sunday afternoons. I sometimes went with my cigar-maker friends to public balls that were given at a large hall on one of the main streets. I learned to take a drink occasionally and paid for quite a number that my friends took; but strong liquors never appealed to my appetite. I drank them only when the company I was in required it, and suffered for it afterwards. On the whole, though I was a bit wild, I can't remember that I ever did anything disgraceful, or, as the usual standard for young men goes, anything to forfeit my claim to respectability.

At one of the first public balls I attended I saw the Pullman car porter who had so kindly assisted me in getting to Jacksonville. I went immediately to one of my factory friends and borrowed fifteen dollars with which to repay the loan my benefactor had made me. After I had given him the money, and was thanking him, I noticed that he wore what was, at least, an exact duplicate of my lamented black and gray tie. It was somewhat worn, but distinct enough for me to trace the same odd design which had first attracted my eye. This was enough to arouse my strongest suspicions, but whether it was sufficient for the law to take cognizance of I did not consider. My astonishment and the ironical humor of the situation drove everything else out of my mind.

These balls were attended by a great variety of people. They were generally given by the waiters of some one of the big hotels, and were often patronized by a number of hotel guests who came to "see the sights." The crowd was always noisy, but good-natured; there was much quadrille dancing, and a strong-lunged man called figures in a voice which did not confine itself to the limits of the hall. It is not worth the while for me to describe in detail how these people acted; they conducted themselves in about the same manner as I have seen other people at similar balls conduct themselves. When one has seen something of the world and human nature he must conclude, after all, that between people in like stations of life there is very little difference the world over.

However, it was at one of these balls that I first saw the cake-walk. There was a contest for a gold watch, to be awarded to the hotel head-waiter receiving the greatest number of votes. There was some dancing while the votes were being counted. Then the floor was cleared for the cake-walk. A half-dozen guests from some of the hotels took seats on the stage to act as judges, and twelve or fourteen couples began to walk for a "sure enough" highly decorated cake, which was in plain evidence. The spectators crowded about the space reserved for the contestants and watched them with interest and excitement. The couples did not walk around in a circle, but in a square, with the men on the inside. The fine points to be considered were the bearing of the men, the precision with which they turned the corners, the grace of the women, and the ease with which they swung around the pivots. The men walked with stately and soldierly step, and the women with considerable grace. The judges arrived at their decision by a process of elimination. The music and the walk continued for some minutes; then both were stopped while the judges conferred, when the walk began again several couples were left out. In this way the contest was finally narrowed down to three or four couples. Then the excitement became intense; there was much partisan cheering as one couple or another would execute a turn in extra elegant style. When the cake was finally awarded the spectators were about evenly divided between those who cheered the winners and those who muttered about the unfairness of the judges. This was the cake-walk in its original form, and it is what the colored performers on the theatrical stage developed into the prancing movements now known all over the world, and which some Parisian critics pronounced the acme of poetic motion.

There are a great many colored people who are ashamed of the cake-walk, but I think they ought to be proud of it. It is my opinion that the colored people of this country have done four things which refute the oft advanced theory that they are an absolutely inferior race, which demonstrate that they have originality and artistic conception; and, what is more, the power of creating that which can influence and appeal universally. The first two of these are the Uncle Remus stories, collected by Joel Chandler Harris, and the Jubilee songs, to which the Fisk singers made the public and the skilled musicians of both America and Europe listen. The other two are ragtime music and the cake-walk. No one who has traveled can question the world-conquering influence of ragtime; and

I do not think it would be an exaggeration to say that in Europe the United States is popularly known better by ragtime than by anything else it has produced in a generation. In Paris they call it American music. The newspapers have already told how the practice of intricate cake walk steps has taken up the time of European royalty and nobility. These are lower forms of art, but they give evidence of a power that will some day be applied to the higher forms. In this measure, at least, and aside from the number of prominent individuals the colored people of the United States have produced, the race has been a world influence; and all of the Indians between Alaska and Patagonia haven't done as much.

Just when I was beginning to look upon Jacksonville as my permanent home, and was beginning to plan about marrying the young school teacher, raising a family, and working in a cigar factory the rest of my life, for some reason, which I do not now remember, the factory at which I worked was indefinitely shut down. Some of the men got work in other factories in town, some decided to go to Key West and Tampa, others made up their minds to go to New York for work. All at once a desire like a fever seized me to see the North again, and I cast my lot with those bound for New York.

CHAPTER VI

We steamed up into New York harbor late one afternoon in spring. The last efforts of the sun were being put forth in turning the waters of the bay to glistening gold; the green islands on either side, in spite of their warlike mountings, looked calm and peaceful; the buildings of the town shone out in a reflected light which gave the city an air of enchantment; and, truly, it is an enchanted spot. New York City is the most fatally fascinating thing in America. She sits like a great witch at the gate of the country, showing her alluring white face, and hiding her crooked hands and feet under the folds of her wide garments,—constantly enticing thousands from far within, and tempting those who come from across the seas to go no farther. And all these become the victims of her caprice. Some she at once crushes beneath her cruel feet; others she condemns to a fate like that of galley slaves; a few she favors and fondles, riding them high on the bubbles of fortune; then with a sudden breath she blows the bubbles out and laughs mockingly as she watches them fall.

Twice I had passed through it; but this was really my first visit to New York; and as I walked about that evening I began to feel the dread power of the city; the crowds, the lights, the excitement, the gayety and all its subtler stimulating influences began to take effect upon me. My blood ran quicker, and I felt that I was just beginning to live. To some natures this stimulant of life in a great city becomes a thing as binding and necessary as opium is to one addicted to the habit. It becomes their breath of life; they cannot exist outside of it; rather than be deprived of it they are content to suffer hunger, want, pain and misery; they would not exchange even a ragged and wretched condition among the great crowd for any degree of comfort away from it.

As soon as we landed, four of us went directly to a lodging-house in 27th Street, just west of Sixth Avenue. The house was run by a short, stout mulatto man, who was exceedingly talkative and inquisitive. In fifteen minutes he not only knew the history of the past life of each one of us, but had a clearer idea of what we intended to do in the future than we ourselves. He sought this information so much with an air of being very particular as to whom he admitted into his house that we tremblingly answered every question that he asked. When we had become located we went out and got supper; then walked around until about ten o'clock. At that hour we met a couple of young fellows who lived in New York and were known to one of the members of our party. It was suggested we go to a certain place which was known by the proprietor's name. We turned into one of the cross streets and mounted the stoop of a house in about the middle of a block between Sixth and Seventh Avenues. One of the young men whom we had met rang a bell, and a man on the inside cracked the door a couple of inches; then opened it and let us in. We found ourselves in the hallway of what had once been a residence. The front parlor had been converted into a bar, and a half dozen or so of well dressed men were in the room. We went in, and after a general intro-duction had several rounds of beer. In the back parlor a crowd was sitting and standing around the walls of the room watching an exciting and noisy game of pool. I walked back and joined this crowd to watch the game, and principally to get away from the drinking party. The game was really interesting, the players being quite expert, and the excitement was heightened by the bets which were being made on the result. At times the antics and remarks of both players and spectators were amusing. When, at a critical point, a player missed a shot he was deluged by those financially interested in his making it with a flood of epithets synonymous to "chump"; while from the others he would be jeered by such remarks as "Nigger, dat cue ain't no hoe-handle." I noticed that among this class of colored men the word "nigger" was freely used in about the same sense as the word "'fellow," and sometimes as a term of almost endearment; but I soon learned that its use was positively and absolutely prohibited to white men.

I stood watching this pool game until I was called by my friends, who were still in the bar-room, to go upstairs. On the second floor there were two large rooms. From the hall I looked into the one on the front. There was a large, round table in the center, at which five or six men were seated playing poker. The air and conduct here were greatly in contrast to what I had just seen in the pool-room; these men were evidently the aristocrats of the place; they were well, perhaps a hit flashily, dressed and spoke in low modulated voices, frequently using the word "gentlemen"; in fact, they seemed to be practicing a sort of Chesterfieldian politeness towards each other. I was watching these men with a great deal of interest and some degree of admiration, when I was again called by the members of our party, and I followed them on to the back room. There was a door-keeper at this room, and we were admitted only after inspection. When we got inside I saw a crowd of men of all ages and kinds grouped about an old billiard table, regarding some of whom, in supposing them to be white, I made no mistake. At first I did not know what these men were doing; they were using terms that were strange to me. I could hear only a confusion of voices exclaiming, "Shoot the two!" "Shoot the four!" "Fate me!" "Fate me!" "I've got you fated!" "Twenty-five cents he don't turn!" This was the ancient and terribly fascinating game of dice, popularly known as "craps." I, myself, had played pool in Jacksonville; it is a favorite game among cigar-makers, and I had seen others play cards; but here was something new. I edged my way in to the table and stood between one of my new-found New York friends and a tall, slender, black fellow, who was making side bets while the dice were at the other end of the table. My companion explained to me the principles of the game; and they are so simple that they hardly need to be explained twice. The dice came around the table until they reached the man on the other side of the tall, black fellow. He lost, and the latter said, "Gimme the bones." He threw a dollar on the table and said, "Shoot the dollar." His style of play was so strenuous that he had to be allowed plenty of room. He shook the dice high above his head, and each time he threw them on the table he emitted a grunt such as men give when they are putting forth physical exertion with a rhythmic regularity. He frequently whirled completely around on his heels, throwing the dice the entire length of the table, and talking to them as though they were trained animals. He appealed to them in short singsong phrases. "Come dice," he would say. "Little Phoebe," "Little Joe," "Way down yonder in the cornfield." Whether these mystic incantations were efficacious or not I could not say, but, at any rate, his luck was great, and he had what gamblers term "nerve." "Shoot the dollar!" "Shoot the two!" "Shoot the four!" "Shoot the eight!" came from his lips as quickly as the dice turned to his advantage. My companion asked me if I had ever played. I told him no. He said that I ought to try my luck; that everybody won at first. The tall man at my side was waving his arms in the air exclaiming "Shoot the sixteen!" "Shoot the sixteen!" "Fate me!" Whether it was my companion's suggestion or some latent dare-devil strain in my blood which suddenly sprang into activity I do not know; but with a thrill of excitement which went through my whole body I threw a twenty dollar bill on the table and said in a trembling voice, "I fate you."

I could feel that I had gained the attention and respect of everybody in the room, every eye was fixed on me, and the widespread question, "Who is he?" went around. This was gratifying to a certain sense of vanity of which I have never been able to rid myself, and I felt that it was worth the money even if I lost. The tall man with a whirl on his heels and a double grunt threw the dice; four was the number which turned up. This is considered as a hard "point" to make. He redoubled his contortions and his grunts and his pleadings to the dice; but on his third or fourth throw the fateful seven turned up, and I had won. My companion and all my friends shouted to me to follow up my luck. The fever was on me. I seized the dice. My hands were so hot that the bits of bone felt like pieces of ice. I shouted as loudly as I could, "Shoot it all!" but the blood was tingling so about my ears that I could not hear my own voice. I was soon "fated." I threw the dice—seven—I had won. "Shoot it all!" I cried again. There was a pause; the stake was more than one man cared to or could cover. I was finally "fated" by several men taking "a part" of it. I then threw the dice again. Seven. I had won. "Shoot it all!" I shouted excitedly. After a short delay I was "fated." Again I rolled the dice. Eleven. Again I had won. My friends now surrounded me and, much against my inclination, forced me to take down all of the money except five dollars. I tried my luck once more, and threw some small "Point" which I failed to make, and the dice passed on to the next man.

In less than three minutes I had won more than two hundred dollars, a sum which afterwards cost me dearly. I was the hero of the moment, and was soon surrounded by a group of men who expressed admiration for my "nerve" and predicted for me a brilliant future as a gambler. Although at the time I had no thought of becoming a gambler I felt proud of my success. I felt a bit ashamed, too, that I had allowed my friends to persuade me to take down my money so soon. Another set of men also got around me, and begged me for twenty-five or fifty cents to put them back into the game. I gave each of them something. I saw that several of them had on linen, dusters, and as I looked about I noticed that there were perhaps a dozen men in the room similarly clad. I asked the fellow who had been my prompter at the dice table why they dressed in such a manner. He told me that men who had lost all the money and jewelry they possessed, frequently, in an effort to recoup their losses, would gamble away all their outer clothing and even their shoes; and that the proprietor kept on hand a supply of linen dusters for all who were so unfortunate. My informant went on to say that sometimes a fellow would become almost completely dressed and then, by a turn of the dice, would be thrown back into a state of semi-nakedness. Some of them were virtually prisoners and unable to get into the streets for days at a time. They ate at the lunch counter, where their credit was good so long as they were fair gamblers and did not attempt to jump their debts, and they slept around in chairs. They importuned friends and winners to put them back in the game, and kept at it until fortune again smiled on them. I laughed heartily at this, not thinking the day was coming which would find me in the same ludicrous predicament.

On passing downstairs I was told that the third and top floor of the house was occupied by the proprietor. When we passed through the bar I treated everybody in the room,—and that was no small number, for eight or ten had followed us down. Then our party went out. It was now about half-past twelve, but my nerves were at such a tension that I could not endure the mere thought of going to bed. I asked if there was no other place to which we could go; our guides said yes, and suggested that we go to the "Club." We went to Sixth Avenue, walked two blocks, and turned to the west into another street. We stopped in front of a house with three stories and a basement. In the basement was a Chinese Chop-suey restaurant. There was a red lantern at the iron gate to the areaway, inside of which the Chinaman's name was printed. We went up the steps of the stoop, rang the bell, and were admitted without any delay. From the outside the house bore a rather gloomy aspect, the windows being absolutely dark, but within it was a veritable house of mirth. When we had passed through a small vestibule and reached the hallway we heard mingled sounds of music and laughter, the clink of glasses and the pop of bottles. We went into the main room, and I was little prepared for what I saw. The brilliancy of the place, the display of diamond rings, scarf-pins, ear-rings and breast-pins, the big rolls of money that were brought into evidence when drinks were paid for, and the air of gayety that pervaded, all completely dazzled and dazed me. I felt positively giddy, and it was several minutes before I was able to make any clear and definite observations.

We at length secured places at a table in a corner of the room, and as soon as we could attract the attention of one of the busy waiters ordered a round of drinks. When I had somewhat collected my senses I realized that in a large back room into which the main room opened, there was a young fellow singing a song, accompanied on the piano by a short, thick-set, dark man. Between each verse he did some dance steps, which brought forth great applause and a shower of small coins at his feet. After the singer had responded to a rousing encore, the stout man at the piano began to run his fingers up and down the keyboard. This he did in a manner which indicated that he was master of a good deal of technic. Then he began to play; and such playing! I stopped talking to listen. It was music of a kind I had never heard before. It was music that demanded physical response, patting of the feet, drumming of the fingers, or nodding of the head in time with the beat. The barbaric harmonies, the audacious resolutions often consisting of an abrupt jump from one key to another, the intricate rhythms in which the accents fell in the most unexpected places, but in which the beat was never lost, produced a most curious effect. And, too, the player,—the dexterity of his left hand in making rapid octave runs and jumps was little short of marvelous; and, with his right hand, he frequently swept half the keyboard with clean cut chromatics which he fitted in so nicely as never to fail to arouse in his listeners a sort of pleasant surprise at the accomplishment of the feat.

This was ragtime music, then a novelty in New York, and just growing to be a rage which has not yet subsided. It was originated in the questionable resorts about Memphis and St. Louis by Negro piano players, who knew no more of the theory of music than they did of the theory of the universe, but were guided by natural musical instinct and talent. It made its way to Chicago, where it was popular some time before it reached New York. These players often improvised crude and, at times, vulgar words to fit the melodies. This was the beginning of the ragtime song. Several of these improvisations were taken down by white men, the words slightly altered, and published under the names of the arrangers. They sprang into immediate popularity and earned small fortunes, of which the Negro originators got only a few dollars. But I have learned that since that time a number of colored men, of not only musical talent, but training, are writing out their own melodies and words and reaping the reward of their work. I have learned also that they have a large number of white imitators and adulterators.

American musicians, instead of investigating ragtime, attempt to ignore it or dismiss it with a contemptuous word. But that has always been the course of scholasticism in every branch of art. Whatever new thing the people like is pooh-poohed; whatever is popular is spoken of as not worth the while. The fact is, nothing great or enduring, especially in music, has ever sprung full-fledged and unprecedented from the brain of any master; the best that he gives to the world he gathers from the hearts of the people, and runs it through the alembic of his genius. In spite of the bans which musicians and music teachers have placed upon it, the people still demand and enjoy ragtime. One thing cannot be denied; it is music which possesses at least one strong element of greatness; it appeals universally; not only the American, but the English, the French, and even the German people, find delight in it. In fact, there is not a corner of the civilized world in which it is not known, and this proves its originality; for if it were an imitation, the people of Europe, anyhow, would not have found it a novelty. Anyone who doubts that there is a peculiar heel-tickling, smile-provoking, joy-awakening charm in ragtime needs only to hear a skillful performer play the genuine article to be convinced. I believe that it has its place as well as the music which draws from us sighs and tears.

I became so interested in both the music and the player that I left the table where I was sitting, and made my way through the hall into the back room, where I could see as well as hear. I talked to the piano player between the musical numbers, and found out that he was just a natural musician, never having taken a lesson in his life. Not only could he play almost anything he heard, but could accompany singers in songs he had never heard. He had by ear alone, composed some pieces, several of which he played over for me; each of them was properly proportioned and balanced. I began to wonder what this man with such a lavish natural endowment would have done had he been trained. Perhaps he wouldn't have done anything at all; he might have become, at best, a mediocre imitator of the great masters in what they have already done to a finish, or one of the modern innovators who strive after originality by seeing how cleverly they can dodge about through the rules of harmony, and at the same time avoid melody. It is certain that he would not have been so delightful as he was in ragtime.

I sat by watching and listening to this man until I was dragged away by my friends. The place was now almost deserted; only a few stragglers hung on, and they were all the worse for drink. My friends were well up in this class. We passed into the street; the lamps were pale against the sky; day was just breaking. We went home and got into bed. I fell into a fitful sort of sleep with ragtime music ringing continually in my ears.

CHAPTER VII

I shall take advantage of this pause in my narrative to more closely describe the "Club" spoken of in the latter part of the preceding chapter,—to describe it, as I afterwards came to know it, as an habitue. I shall do this, not only because of the direct influence it had on my life, but also because it was at that time the most famous place of its kind in New York, and was well known to both white and colored people of certain classes.

I have already stated that in the basement of the house there was a Chinese restaurant. The Chinaman who kept it did an exceptionally good business; for chop-suey was a favorite dish among the frequenters of the place. It is a food that, somehow, has the power of absorbing alcoholic liquors that have been taken into the stomach. I have heard men claim that they could sober up on chop-suey. Perhaps that accounted, in some degree, for its popularity. On the main floor there were two large rooms, a parlor about thirty feet in length and a large square back room into which the parlor opened. The floor of the parlor was carpeted; small tables and chairs were arranged about the room; the windows were draped with lace curtains, and the walls were literally covered with photographs or lithographs of every colored man in America who had ever "done anything." There were pictures of Frederick Douglass and of Peter Jackson, of all the lesser lights of the prize-fighting ring, of all the famous jockeys and the stage celebrities, down to the newest song and dance team. The most of these photographs were autographed and, in a sense, made a really valuable collection. In the back room there was a piano; and tables were placed around the wall. The floor was bare and the center was left vacant for singers, dancers and others who entertained the patrons. In a closet in this room which jutted out into the hall the proprietor kept his buffet. There was no open bar, because the place had no liquor license. In this back room the tables were sometimes pushed aside, and the floor given over to general dancing. The front room on the next floor was a sort of private party room; a back room on the same floor contained no furniture, and was devoted to the use of new and ambitions performers. In this room song and dance teams practiced their steps, acrobatic teams practiced their tumbles, and many other kinds of "acts" rehearsed their "turns." The other rooms of the house were used as sleeping apartments.

No gambling was allowed, and the conduct of the place was surprisingly orderly. It was, in short, a center of colored bohemians and sports. Here the great prize fighters were wont to come, the famous jockeys, the noted minstrels, whose names and faces were familiar on every bill-board in the country; and these drew a multitude of those who love to dwell in the shadow of greatness. There were then no organizations giving performances of such order as are now given by several colored companies; that was because no manager could imagine that audiences would pay to see Negro performers in any other rôle than that of

Mississippi River roustabouts; but there was lots of talent and ambition. I often heard the younger and brighter men discussing the time when they would compel the public to recognize that they could do something more than grin and cut pigeon wings.

Sometimes one or two of the visiting stage professionals, after being sufficiently urged, would go into the back room, and take the places of the regular amateur entertainers, but they were very sparing with these favors, and the patrons regarded them as special treats. There was one man, a minstrel, who, whenever he responded to a request to "do something," never essayed anything below a reading from Shakespeare. How well he read I do not know, but he greatly impressed me; and I can, at least, say that he had a voice which strangely stirred those who heard it. Here was a man who made people laugh at the size of his mouth, while he carried in his heart a burning ambition to be a tragedian; and so after all he did play a part in a tragedy.

These notables of the ring, the turf and the stage, drew to the place crowds of admirers, both white and colored. Whenever one of them came in there were awe-inspired whispers from those who knew him by sight, in which they enlightened those around them as to his identity, and hinted darkly at their great intimacy with the noted one. Those who were on terms of approach immediately showed their privilege over others less fortunate by gathering around their divinity. I was, at first, among those who dwelt in darkness. Most of these celebrities I had never heard of. This made me an object of pity among many of my new associates. I, however, soon learned to fake a knowledge for the benefit of those who were greener than I; and, finally, I became personally acquainted with the majority of the famous personages who came to the "Club."

A great deal of money was spent here; so many of the patrons were men who earned large sums. I remember one night a dapper little brown-skinned fellow was pointed out to me, and I was told that he was the most popular jockey of the day, and that he earned $12,000 a year. This latter statement I couldn't doubt, for with my own eyes I saw him spending at about that rate. For his friends and those who were introduced to him he bought nothing but wine;—in the sporting circle, "wine" means champagne—and paid for it at five dollars a quart. He sent a quart to every table in the place with his compliments; and on the table at which he and his party were seated there were more than a dozen bottles. It was the custom at the "Club" for the waiter not to remove the bottles when champagne was being drunk until the party had finished. There were reasons for this; it advertised the brand of wine, it advertised that the party was drinking wine, and advertised how much they had bought. This jockey had won a great race that day, and he was rewarding his admirers for the homage they paid him, all of which he accepted with a fine air of condescension.

Besides the people I have just been describing there was at the place almost every night one or two parties of white people, men and women, who were out sight-seeing, or slumming. They generally came in cabs; some of them would stay only for a few minutes, while others sometimes stayed until morning. There was also another set of white people who came frequently; it was made up of variety performers and others who delineated darky characters; they came to get their imitatations first hand from the Negro entertainers they saw there.

There was still another set of white patrons, composed of women; these were not occasional visitors, but five or six of them were regular habitues. When I first saw them I was not sure that they were white. In the first place, among the many colored women who came to the "Club" there were several just as fair; and, secondly, I always saw these women in company with colored men. They were all good-looking and well dressed, and seemed to be women of some education. One of these in particular attracted my attention; she was an exceedingly beautiful woman of perhaps thirty-five; she had glistening copper-colored hair, very white skin and eyes very much like Du Maurier's conception of Trilby's "twin gray stars." When I came to know her I found that she was a woman of considerable culture; she had traveled in Europe, spoke French, and played the piano well. She was always dressed elegantly, but in absolute good taste. She always came to the "Club" in a cab, and was soon joined by a well set up, very black young fellow. He was always faultlessly dressed; one of the most exclusive tailors in New York made his clothes, and he wore a number of diamonds in about as good taste as they could be worn by a man. I learned that she paid for his clothes and his diamonds. I learned, too, that he was not the only one of his kind. More that I learned would be better suited to a book on social phenomena than to a narrative of my life. This woman was known at the "Club" as the rich widow. She -went by a very aristocratic sounding name, which corresponded to her appearance. I shall never forget how hard it was for me to get over my feelings of surprise, perhaps more than surprise, at seeing her with her black companion; somehow I never exactly enjoyed the sight. I have devoted so much time to this pair, the "widow" and her companion, because it was through them that another decided turn was brought about in my life.

CHAPTER VIII

On the day following our night at the "Club" we slept until late in the afternoon; so late that beginning of search for work was entirely out of the question. This did not cause me much worry, for I had more than three hundred dollars, and New York had impressed me as a place where there was lots of money and not much difficulty in getting it. It is needless to inform my readers that I did not long hold this opinion. We got out of the house about dark, went round to a restaurant on Sixth Avenue and ate something, then walked around for a couple of hours. I finally suggested that we visit the same places we had been in the night before. Following my suggestion we started first to the gambling house. The man on the door let us in without any question; I accredited this to my success of the night before. We went straight to the "crap" room, and I at once made my way to a table, where I was rather flattered by the murmur of recognition which went around. I played in up and down luck for three or four hours; then, worn with nervous excitement, quit, having lost about fifty dollars. But I was so strongly possessed with the thought that I would make up my losses the next time I played that I left the place with a light heart.

When we got into the street our party was divided against itself; two were for going home at once and getting to bed. They gave as a reason that we were to get up early and look for jobs. I think the real reason was that they had each lost several dollars in the game. I lived to learn that in the world of sport all men win alike but lose differently; and so gamblers are rated, not by the way in which they win, but by the way in which they lose. Some men lose with a careless smile, recognizing that losing is a part of the game; others curse their luck and rail at fortune; and others, still, lose sadly; after each such experience they are swept by a wave of reform; they resolve to stop gambling and be good. When in this frame of mind it would take very little persuasion to lead them into a prayer-meeting. Those in the first class are looked upon with admiration; those in the second class are merely commonplace; while those in the third are regarded with contempt. I believe these distinctions hold good in all the ventures of life. After some minutes one of my friends and I succeeded in convincing the other two that a while at the "Club" would put us all in better spirits; and they consented to go on our promise not to stay longer than an hour. We found the place crowded, and the same sort of thing going on which we had seen the night before. I took a seat at once by the side of the piano player, and was soon lost to everything else except the novel charm of the music. I watched the performer with the idea of catching the trick; and, during one of his intermissions, I took his place at the piano and made an attempt to imitate him, but even my quick ear and ready fingers were unequal to the task on first trial.

We did not stay at the "Club" very long, but went home to bed in order to be up early the next day. We had no difficulty in finding work, and my third morning in New York found me at a table rolling cigars. I worked steadily for some weeks, at the same time spending my earnings between the "crap" game and the "Club." Making cigars became more and more irksome to me; perhaps my more congenial work as a "reader" had unfitted me for work at the table. And, too, the late hours I was keeping made such a sedentary occupation almost beyond the powers of will and endurance. I often found it hard to keep my eyes open and sometimes had to get up and move around to keep from falling asleep. I began to miss whole days from the factory, days on which I was compelled to stay at home and sleep.

My luck at the gambling table was varied; sometimes I was fifty to a hundred dollars ahead, and at other times I had to borrow money from my fellow workmen to settle my room rent and pay for my meals. Each night after leaving the dice game I went to the "Club" to hear the music and watch the gayety. If I had won, this was in accord with my mood; if I had lost, it made me forget. I at last realized that making cigars for a living and gambling for a living could not both be carried on at the same time, and I resolved to give up the cigar-making. This resolution led me into a life which held me bound more than a year. During that period my regular time for going to bed was somewhere between four and six o'clock in the mornings. I got up late in the afternoons, walked about a little, then went to the gambling house or the "Club." My New York was limited to ten blocks; the boundaries were Sixth Avenue from Twenty-third to Thirty-third Streets, with the cross streets one block to the west. Central Park was a distant forest, and the lower part of the city a foreign land. I look back upon the life I then led with a shudder when I think what would have been had I not escaped it. But had I not escaped it, I would have been no more unfortunate than are many young colored men who come to New York. During that dark period I became acquainted with a score of bright, intelligent young fellows who had come up to the great city with high hopes and ambitions, and who had fallen under the spell of this under life, a spell they could not throw off. There was one popularly known as "the doctor"; he had had two years in the Harvard Medical School; but here he was, living this gas-light life, his will and moral sense so enervated and deadened that it was impossible for him to break away. I do not doubt that the same thing is going on now, but I have rather sympathy than censure for these victims, for I know how easy it is to slip into a slough from which it takes a herculean effort to leap.

I regret that I cannot contrast my views of life among colored people of New York; but the truth is, during my entire stay in this city I did not become acquainted with a single respectable family. I knew that there were several colored men worth a hundred or so thousand dollars each, and some families who proudly dated their free ancestry back a half-dozen generations. I also learned that in Brooklyn there lived quite a large colony in comfortable homes, most of which they owned; but at no point did my life come in contact with theirs.

In my gambling experiences I passed through all the states and conditions that a gambler is heir to. Some days found me able to peel ten and twenty dollar bills from a roll, and others found me clad in a linen duster and carpet slippers. I finally caught up another method of earning money, and so did not have to depend entirely upon the caprices of fortune at the gaming table. Through continually listening to the music at the "Club," and through my own previous training, my natural talent and perseverance, I developed into a remarkable player of ragtime; indeed, I had the name at that time of being the best ragtime player in New York. I brought all my knowledge of classic music to bear and, in so doing, achieved some novelties which pleased and even astonished my listeners. It was I who first made ragtime transcriptions of familiar classic selections. I used to play Mendelssohn's "Wedding March" in a manner that never failed to arouse enthusiasm among the patrons of the "Club." Very few nights passed during which I was not asked to play it. It was no secret that the great increase in slumming visitors was due to my playing. By mastering ragtime I gained several things; first of all, I gained the title of professor. I was known as the "professor" as long as I remained in that world. Then, too, I gained the means of earning a rather fair livelihood. This work took up much of my time and kept me almost entirely away from the gambling table. Through it I also gained a friend who was the means by which I escaped from this lower world. And, finally, I secured a wedge which has opened to me more doors and made me a welcome guest than my playing of Beethoven and Chopin could ever have done.

The greater part of the money I now began to earn came through the friend to whom I alluded in the foregoing paragraph. Among the other white "slummers" there came into the "Club" one night a clean cut, slender, but athletic looking man, who would have been taken for a youth had it not been for the tinge of gray about his temples. He was clean shaven, had regular features, and all of his movements bore the indefinable but unmistakable stamp of culture. He spoke to no one, but sat languidly puffing cigarettes and sipping a glass of beer. He was the center of a great deal of attention, all of the old timers were wondering who he was. When I had finished playing he called a waiter and by him sent me a five dollar bill. For about a month after that he was at the "Club" one or two nights each week, and each time after I had played he gave me five dollars. One night he sent for me to come to his table; he asked me several questions about myself; then told me that he had an engagement which he wanted me to fill. He gave me a card containing his address and asked me to be there on a certain night.

I was on hand promptly, and found that he was giving a dinner in his own apartments to a party of ladies and gentlemen, and that I was expected to furnish the musical entertainment. When the grave, dignified man at the door let me in, the place struck me as being almost dark, my eyes had been so accustomed to the garish light of the "Club." He took my coat and hat, bade me take a seat, and went to tell his master that I had come. When my eyes were adjusted to the soft light I saw that I was in the midst of elegance and luxury in such a degree as I had never seen; but not the elegance which makes one ill at ease. As I sank into a great chair the subdued tone, the delicately sensuous harmony of my surroundings drew from me a deep sigh of relief and comfort. How long the man was gone I do not know; but I was startled by a voice saying, "Come this way, if you please, sir," and I saw him standing by my chair. I had been asleep; and I awoke very much confused and a little ashamed, because I did not know how many times he may have called me. I followed him through into the dining-room, where the butler was putting the finishing touches to a table which already looked like a big jewel. The doorman turned me over to the butler, and I passed with the butler on back to where several waiters were busy polishing and assorting table utensils. Without being asked whether I was hungry or not, I was placed at a table and given something to eat. Before I had finished eating I heard the laughter and talk of the guests who were arriving. Soon afterwards I was called in to begin my work.

I passed in to where the company was gathered, and went directly to the piano. According to a suggestion from the host I began with classic music. During the first number there was absolute quiet and appreciative attention, and when I had finished I was given a round of generous applause. After that the talk and the laughter began to grow until the music was only an accompaniment to the chatter. This, however, did not disconcert me as it once would have done, for I had become accustomed to playing in the midst of uproarious noise. As the guests began to pay less attention to me I was enabled to pay more to them. There were about a dozen of them. The men ranged in appearance from a girlish looking youth to a big grizzled man whom everybody addressed as "Judge." None of the women appeared to be under thirty, but each of them struck me as being handsome. I was not long in finding out that they were all decidedly blasé. Several of the women smoked cigarettes, and with a careless grace which showed they were used to the habit. Occasionally a "damn it!" escaped from the lips of some one of them, but in such a charming way as to rob it of all vulgarity. The most notable thing which I observed was that the reserve of the host increased in direct proportion with the hilarity of his guests. I thought that there was something going wrong which displeased him. I afterwards learned that it was his habitual manner on such occasions. He seemed to take cynical delight in watching and studying others indulging in excess. His guests were evidently accustomed to his rather non-participating attitude, for it did not seem in any degree to dampen their spirits. When dinner was served the piano was moved and the door left open, so that the company might hear the music while eating. At a word from the host I struck up one of my liveliest ragtime pieces. The effect was perhaps surprising, even to the host; the ragtime music came very near spoiling the party so far as eating the dinner was concerned. As soon as I began the conversation stopped suddenly. It was a pleasure to me to watch the expression of astonishment and delight that grew on the faces of everybody. These were people,—and they represented a large class,—who were ever expecting to find happiness in novelty, each day restlessly exploring and exhausting every resource of this great city that might possibly furnish a new sensation or awaken a fresh emotion, and who were always grateful to anyone who aided them in their quest. Several of the women left the table and gathered about the piano. They watched my fingers, asked what kind of music it was that I was playing, where I had learned it and a host of other questions. It was only by being repeatedly called back to the table that they were induced to finish their dinner. When the guests arose I struck up my ragtime transcription of Mendelssohn's "Wedding March," playing it with terrific chromatic octave runs in the base. This raised everybody's spirits to the highest point of gayety, and the whole company involuntarily and unconsciously did an impromptu cake-walk. From that time on until the time of leaving they kept me so busy that my arms ached. I obtained a little respite when the girlish looking youth and one or two of the ladies sang several songs, but after each of these it was, "back to ragtime."

In leaving, the guests were enthusiastic in telling the host that he had furnished them the most unique entertainment they had "ever" enjoyed. When they had gone, my millionaire friend,—for he was reported to be a millionaire,—said to me with a smile, "Well, I have given them something they've never had before." After I had put on my coat and was ready to leave he made me take a glass of wine; he then gave me a cigar and twenty dollars in bills. He told me that he would give me lots of work, his only stipulation being that I should not play any engagements such as I had just filled for him, except by his instructions. I readily accepted the proposition, for I was sure that I could not be the loser by such a contract.

I afterwards played for him at many dinners and parties of one kind or another. Occasionally he "loaned" me to some of his friends. And, too, I often played for him alone at his apartments. At such times he was quite a puzzle to me until I became accustomed to his manners. He would sometimes sit for three or four hours hearing me play, his eyes almost closed, making scarcely a motion except to light a fresh cigarette, and never commenting one way or another on the music. At first, I used sometimes to think that he had fallen asleep and would pause in playing. The stopping of the music always aroused him enough to tell me to play this or that; and I soon learned that my task was not to be considered finished until he got up from his chair and said, "That will do." The man's powers of endurance in listening often exceeded mine in performing—yet I am not sure that he was always listening. At times I became so oppressed with fatigue and sleepiness that it took almost superhuman effort to keep my fingers going; in fact, I believe I sometimes did so while dozing. During such moments, this man sitting there so mysteriously silent, almost hid in a cloud of heavy-scented smoke, filled me with a sort of unearthly terror. He seemed to be some grim, mute, but relentless tyrant, possessing over me a supernatural power which he used to drive me on mercilessly to exhaustion. But these feelings came very rarely; besides, he paid me so liberally I could forget much. There at length grew between us a familiar and warm relationship; and I am sure he had a decided personal liking for me. On my part, I looked upon him at that time as about all a man could wish to be.

The "Club" still remained my headquarters, and when I was not playing for my good patron I was generally to be found there. However, I no longer depended on playing at the "Club" to earn my living; I rather took rank with the visiting celebrities and, occasionally, after being sufficiently urged, would favor my old and new admirers with a number or two. I say, without any egotistic pride, that among my admirers were several of the best looking women who frequented the place, and who made no secret of the fact that they admired me as much as they did my playing. Among these was the "widow"; indeed, her attentions became so marked that one of my friends warned me to beware of her black companion, who was generally known as a "bad man." He said there was much more reason to be careful because the pair had lately quarreled, and had not been together at the "Club" for some nights. This warning greatly impressed me and I resolved to stop the affair before it should go any further; but the woman was so beautiful that my native gallantry and delicacy would not allow me to repulse her; my finer feelings entirely overcame my judgment. The warning also opened my eyes sufficiently to see that though my artistic temperament and skill made me interesting and attractive to the woman, she was, after all, using me only to excite the jealousy of her companion and revenge herself upon him. It was this surly black despot who held sway over her deepest emotions.

One night, shortly afterwards, I went into the "Club" and saw the "widow" sitting at a table in company with another woman. She at once beckoned for me to come to her. I went, knowing that I was committing worse than folly. She ordered a quart of champagne and insisted that I sit down and drink with her. I took a chair on the opposite side of the table and began to sip a glass of the wine. Suddenly I noticed by an expression on the "widow's" face that something had occurred. I instinctively glanced around and saw that her companion had just entered. His ugly look completely frightened me. My back was turned to him, but by watching the "widow's" eyes I judged that he was pacing back and forth across the room. My feelings were far from comfortable; I expected every moment to feel a blow on my head. She, too, was very nervous; she was trying hard to appear unconcerned, but could not succeed in hiding her real feelings. I decided that it was best to get out of such a predicament even at the expense of appearing cowardly, and I made a motion to rise. Just as I partly turned in my chair, I saw the black fellow approaching; he walked directly to our table and leaned over. The "Widow" evidently feared he was going to strike her, and she threw back her head. Instead of striking her he whipped out a revolver and fired; the first shot went straight into her throat. There were other shots fired, but how many I do not know; for the first knowledge I had of my surroundings and actions was that I was rushing through the chop-suey restaurant into the street. Just which streets I followed when I got outside I do not know, but I think I must have gone towards Eighth Avenue, then down towards Twenty-third Street and across towards Fifth Avenue. I traveled not by sight, but instinctively. I felt like one fleeing in a horrible nightmare.

How long and far I walked I cannot tell; but on Fifth Avenue, under a light, I passed a cab containing a solitary occupant, who called to me, and I recognized the voice and face of my millionaire friend. He stopped the cab and asked, "What on earth are you doing strolling in this part of the town?" For answer I got into the cab and related to him all that had happened. He reassured me by saying that no charge of any kind could be brought against me; then added, "But, of course, you don't want to he mixed up in such an affair." He directed the driver to turn around and go into the park, and then went on to say, "I decided last night that I'd go to Europe to-morrow. I think I'll take you along instead of Walter." Walter was his valet. It was settled that I should go to his apartments for the rest of the night and sail with him in the morning.

We drove around through the park, exchanging only an occasional word. The cool air somewhat calmed my nerves and I lay back and closed my eyes; but still I could see that beautiful white throat with the ugly wound. The jet of blood pulsing from it had placed an indelible red stain on my memory.

CHAPTER IX

I did not feel at ease until the ship was well out of New York harbor; and, notwithstanding the repeated reassurances of my millionaire friend and my own knowledge of the facts in the case, I somehow could not rid myself of the sentiment that I was, in a great degree, responsible for the widow's tragic end. We had brought most of the morning papers aboard with us, but my great fear of seeing my name in connection with the killing would not permit me to read the accounts, although, in one of the papers, I did look at the picture of the victim, which did not in the least resemble her. This morbid state of mind, together with seasickness, kept me miserable for three or four days. At the end of that time my spirits began to revive, and I took an interest in the ship, my fellow passengers, and the voyage in general. On the second or third day out we passed several spouting whales; but I could not arouse myself to make the effort to go to the other side of the ship to see them. A little later we ran in close proximity to a large iceberg. I was curious enough to get up and look at it, and I was fully repaid for my pains. The sun was shining full upon it, and it glistened like a mammoth diamond, cut with a million facets. As we passed it constantly changed its shape; at each different angle of vision it assumed new and astonishing forms of beauty. I watched it through a pair of glasses, seeking to verify my early conception of an iceberg—in the geographies of my grammar-school days the pictures of icebergs always included a stranded polar bear, standing desolately upon one of the snowy crags. I looked for the bear, but if he was there he refused to put himself on exhibition.

It was not, however, until the morning that we entered the harbor of Havre that I was able to shake off my gloom. Then the strange sights, the chatter in an unfamiliar tongue and the excitement of landing and passing the customs officials caused me to forget completely the events of a few days before. Indeed, I grew so light-hearted that when I caught my first sight of the train which was to take us to Paris, I enjoyed a hearty laugh. The toy-looking engine, the stuffy little compartment cars with tiny, old-fashioned wheels, struck me as being extremely funny. But before we reached Paris my respect for our train rose considerably. I found that the "tiny" engine made remarkably fast time, and that the old-fashioned wheels ran very smoothly. I even began to appreciate the "stuffy" cars for their privacy. As I watched the passing scenery from the car window it seemed too beautiful to be real. The bright-colored houses against the green background impressed me as the work of some idealistic painter. Before we arrived in Paris there was awakened in my heart a love for France which continued to grow stronger, a love which today makes that country for me the one above all others to be desired.

We rolled into the station Saint Lazare about four o'clock in the afternoon, and drove immediately to the Hotel Continental. My benefactor, humoring my curiosity and enthusiasm, which seemed to please him very much, suggested that we take a short walk before dinner. We stepped out of the hotel and turned to the right into the Rue de Rivoli. When the vista of the Place de la Concorde and the Champs Elysées suddenly burst on me I could hardly credit my own eyes. I shall attempt no such superogatory task as a description of Paris. I wish only to give briefly the impressions which that wonderful city made upon me. It impressed me as the perfect and perfectly beautiful city; and even after I had been there for some time, and seen not only its avenues and palaces, but its most squalid alleys and hovels, this impression was not weakened. Paris became for me a charmed spot, and whenever I have returned there I have fallen under the spell, a spell which compels admiration for all of its manners and customs and justification of even its follies and sins.

We walked a short distance up the Champs Elysées and, sat for a while in chairs along the sidewalk, watching the passing crowds on foot and in carriages. It was with reluctance that I went back to the hotel for dinner. After dinner we went to one of the summer theaters, and after the performance my friend took me to a large café on one of the grand boulevards. Here it was that I had my first glimpse of the French life of popular literature, so different from real French life. There were several hundred people, men and women, in the place drinking, smoking, talking, and listening to the music. My millionaire friend and I took seats at a table where we sat smoking and watching the crowd. It was not long before we were joined by two or three good-looking, well-dressed young women. My friend talked to them in French and bought drinks for the whole party. I tried to recall my high school French, but the effort availed me little. I could stammer out a few phrases, but, very naturally, could not understand a word that was said to me. We stayed at the café a couple of hours, then went back to the hotel. The next day we spent several hours in the shops and at the tailors. I had no clothes except what I had been able to gather together at my benefactor's apartments the night before we sailed. He bought me the same kind of clothes which he himself wore, and that was the best; and he treated me in every way as he dressed me, as an equal, not as a servant. In fact, I don't think anyone could have guessed that such a relation existed. My duties were light and few, and he was a man full of life and vigor, who rather enjoyed doing things for himself. He kept me supplied with money far beyond what ordinary wages would have amounted to. For the first two weeks we were together almost constantly, seeing the sights, sights old to him, but from which he seemed to get new pleasure in showing them to me. During the day we took in the places of interest, and at night the theaters and cafés. This sort of life appealed to me as ideal, and I asked him one day how long he intended to stay in Paris. He answered, "Oh, until I get tired of it." I could not understand how that could ever happen. As it was, including several short trips to the Mediterranean, to Spain, to Brussels, and to Ostend, we did remain there fourteen or fifteen months. We stayed at the Hotel Continental about two months of this time. Then my millionaire took apartments, hired a piano, and lived almost the same life he lived in New York. He entertained a great deal, some of the parties being a good deal more blasé than the New

York ones. I played for the guests at all of them with an effect which to relate would be but a tiresome repetition to the reader. I played not only for the guests, but continued, as I used to do in New York, to play often for the host when he was alone. This man of the world, who grew weary of everything, and was always searching for something new, appeared never to grow tired of my music; he seemed to take it as a drug. He fell into a habit which caused me no little annoyance; sometimes he would come in during the early hours of the morning, and finding me in bed asleep, would wake me up and ask me to play something. This, so far as I can remember, was my only hardship during my whole stay with him in Europe.

After the first few weeks spent in sight-seeing, I had a great deal of time left to myself; my friend was often I did not know where. When not with him I spent the day nosing about all the curious nooks and corners of Paris; of this I never grew tired. At night I usually went to some theater, but always ended up at the big café on the Grand Boulevards. I wish the reader to know that it was not alone the gayety which drew me there; aside from that I had a laudable purpose. I had purchased an English-French conversational dictionary, and I went there every night to take a language lesson. I used to get three or four of the young women who frequented the place at a table and buy beer and cigarettes for them. In return I received my lesson. I got more than my money's worth; for they actually compelled me to speak the language. This, together with reading the papers every day, enabled me within a few months to express myself fairly well, and, before I left Paris, to have more than an ordinary command of French. Of course, every person who goes to Paris could not dare to learn French in this manner, but I can think of no easier or quicker way of doing it. The acquiring of another foreign language awoke me to the fact that with a little effort I could secure an added accomplishment as fine and as valuable as music; so I determined to make myself as much of a linguist as possible. I bought a Spanish newspaper every day in order to freshen my memory on that language, and, for French, devised what was, so far as I knew, an original system of study. I compiled a list which I termed "Three hundred necessary words." These I thoroughly committed to memory, also the conjugation of the verbs which were included in the list. I studied these words over and over, much like children of a couple of generations ago studied the alphabet. I also practiced a set of phrases like the following: "How?" "What did you say?" "What does the word —— mean?" "I understand all you say except ——." "Please repeat." "What do you call ——?" "How do you say ——?" These I called my working sentences. In an astonishingly short time I reached the point where the language taught itself,—where I learned to speak merely by speaking. This point is the place which students taught foreign languages in our schools and colleges find great difficulty in reaching. I think the main trouble is that they learn too much of a language at a time. A French child with a vocabulary of two hundred words can express more spoken ideas than a student of French can with a knowledge of two thousand. A small vocabulary, the smaller the better, which embraces the common, everyday-used ideas, thoroughly mastered, is the key to a language. When that much is acquired the vocabulary can be increased simply by talking. And it is easy. Who cannot commit three hundred words to memory? Later I tried my method, if I may so term it, with German, and found that it worked in the same way.

I spent a good many evenings at the Grand Opera. The music there made me strangely reminiscent of my life in Connecticut, it was an atmosphere in which I caught a fresh breath of my boyhood days and early youth. Generally, in the morning, after I had attended a performance, I would sit at the piano and for a couple of hours play the music which I used to play in my mother's little parlor.

One night I went to hear "Faust." I got into my seat just as the lights went down for the first act. At the end of the act I noticed that my neighbor on the left was a young girl. I cannot describe her either as to feature, color of her hair, or of her eyes; she was so young, so fair, so ethereal, that I felt to stare at her would be a violation; yet I was distinctly conscious of her beauty. During the intermission she spoke English in a low voice to a gentleman and a lady who sat in the seats to her left, addressing them as father and mother. I held my programme as though studying it, but listened to catch every sound of her voice. Her observations on the performance and the audience were so fresh and naïve as to be almost amusing. I gathered that she was just out of school, and that this was her first trip to Paris. I occasionally stole a glance at her, and each time I did so my heart leaped into my throat. Once I glanced beyond to the gentleman who sat next to her. My glance immediately turned into a stare. Yes, there he was, unmistakably, my father! looking hardly a day older than when I had seen him some ten years before. What a strange coincidence! What should I say to him? What would he say to me? Before I had recovered from my first surprise there came another shock in the realization that the beautiful, tender girl at my side was my sister. Then all the springs of affection in my heart, stopped since my mother's death, burst out in fresh and terrible torrents, and I could have fallen at her feet and worshiped her. They were singing the second act, but I did not hear the music. Slowly the desolate loneliness of my position became clear to me. I knew that I could not speak, but I would have given a part of my life to touch her hand with mine and call her sister. I sat through the opera until I could stand it no longer. I felt that I was suffocating. Valentine's love seemed like mockery, and I felt an almost ·uncontrollable impulse to rise up and scream to the audience, "Here, here in your very midst, is a tragedy, a real tragedy!" This impulse grew so strong that I became afraid of myself, and in the darkness of one of the scenes I stumbled out of the theater. I walked aimlessly about for an hour or so, my feelings divided between a desire to weep and a desire to curse. I finally took a cab and went from café to café, and for one of the very few times in my life drank myself into a stupor.

It was unwelcome news for me when my benefactor—I could not think of him as employer—informed me that he was at last tired of Paris. This news gave me, I think, a passing doubt as to his sanity. I had enjoyed life in Paris, and, taking all things into consideration, enjoyed it wholesomely. One thing which greatly contributed to my enjoyment was the fact that I was an American. Americans are immensely popular in Paris; and this is not due solely to the fact that they spend lots of money there; for they spend just as much or more in London, and in the latter city they are merely tolerated because they do spend. The Londoner seems to think that Americans are people whose only claim to be classed as civilized is that they have money, and the regrettable thing about that is that the money is not English. But the French are more logical and freer from prejudices than the British; so the difference of attitude is easily explained. Only once in Paris did I have cause to blush for my American citizenship. I had become quite friendly with a young man from Luxembourg whom I had met at the big café. He was a stolid, slow-witted fellow, but, as we say, with a heart of gold. He and I grew attached to each other and were together frequently. He was a great admirer of the United States and never grew tired of talking to me about the country and asking for information. It was his intention to try his fortune there some day. One night he asked me in a tone of voice which indicated that he expected an authoritative denial of an ugly rumor, "Did they really burn a man alive in the United States?" I never knew what I stammered out to him as an answer. I should have felt relieved if I could even have said to him, "Well, only one."

When we arrived in London my sadness at leaving Paris was turned into despair. After my long stay in the French capital, huge, ponderous, massive London seemed to me as ugly a thing as man could contrive to make. I thought of Paris as a beauty spot on the face of the earth, and of London as a big freckle. But soon London's massiveness, I might say its very ugliness, began to impress me. I began to experience that sense of grandeur which one feels when he looks at a great mountain or a mighty river. Beside London Paris becomes a toy, a pretty plaything. And I must own that before I left the world's metropolis I discovered much there that was beautiful. The beauty in and about London is entirely different from that in and about Paris; and I could not but admit that the beauty of the French city seemed hand-made, artificial, as though set up for the photographer's camera, everything nicely adjusted so as not to spoil the picture; while that of the English city was rugged, natural and fresh.

How these two cities typify the two peoples who built them! Even the sound of their names express a certain racial difference. Paris is the concrete expression of the gayety, regard for symmetry, love of art and, I might well add, of the morality of the French people. London stands for the conservatism, the solidarity, the utilitarianism and, I might well add, the hypocrisy of the Anglo-Saxon. It may sound odd to speak of the morality of the French, if not of the hypocrisy of the English; but this seeming paradox impressed me as a deep truth. I saw many things in Paris which were immoral according to English standards, but the absence of hypocrisy, the absence of the spirit to do the thing if it might only be done in secret, robbed these very immoralities of the damning influence of the same evils in London. I have walked along the terrace cafés of Paris and seen hundreds of men and women sipping their wine and beer, without observing a sign of drunkenness. As they drank, they chatted and laughed and watched the passing crowds; the drinking seemed to be a secondary thing. This I have witnessed, not only in the cafés along the Grand Boulevards, but in the out-of-way places patronized by the working classes. In London I have seen in the "Pubs" men and women crowded in stuffy little compartments, drinking seemingly only for the pleasure of swallowing as much as they could hold. I have seen there women from eighteen to eighty, some in tatters, and some clutching babes in their arms, drinking the heavy English ales and whiskies served to them by women. In the whole scene, not one ray of brightness, not one flash of gayety, only maudlin joviality or grim despair. And I have thought, if some men and women will drink—and it is certain that some will—is it not better that they do so under the open sky, in the fresh air, than huddled together in some close, smoky room? There is a sort of frankness about the evils of Paris which robs them of much of the seductiveness of things forbidden, and with that frankness goes a certain cleanliness of thought belonging to things not hidden. London will do whatever Paris does, provided exterior morals are not shocked. As a result, Paris has the appearance only of being the more immoral city. The difference may be summed up in this: Paris practices its sins as lightly as it does its religion, while London practices both very seriously.

I should not neglect to mention what impressed me most forcibly during my stay in London. It was not St. Paul's nor the British Museum nor Westminster Abbey. It was nothing more or less than the simple phrase "Thank you," or sometimes more elaborated, "Thank you very kindly, sir." I was continually surprised by the varied uses to which it was put; and, strange to say; its use as an expression of politeness seemed more limited than any other. One night I was in a cheap music hall and accidentally humped into a waiter who was carrying a tray-load of beer, almost bringing him to several shillings' worth of grief. To my amazement he righted himself and said, "Thank ye, sir," and left me wondering whether he meant that he thanked me for not completely spilling his beer, or that he would thank me for keeping out of his way.

I also found cause to wonder upon what ground the English accuse Americans of corrupting the language by introducing slang words. I think I heard more and more different kinds of slang during my few weeks' stay in London than in my whole "tenderloin" life in New York. But I suppose the English feel that the language is theirs, and that they may do with it as they please without at the same time allowing that privilege to others.

My "millionaire" was not so long in growing tired of London as of Paris. After a stay of six or eight weeks we went across into Holland. Amsterdam was a great surprise to me. I had always thought of Venice as the city of canals; but it had never entered my mind that I should find similar conditions in a Dutch town. I don't suppose the comparison goes far beyond the fact that there are canals in both cities—I have never seen Venice—but Amsterdam struck me as being extremely picturesque. From Holland we went to Germany, where we spent five or six months, most of the time in Berlin. I found Berlin more to my taste than London, and occasionally I had to admit that in some things it was superior to Paris.

In Berlin I especially enjoyed the orchestral concerts, and I attended a large number of them. I formed the acquaintance of a good many musicians, several of whom spoke of my playing in high terms. It was in Berlin that my inspiration was renewed. One night my "millionaire" entertained a party of men composed of artists, musicians, writers and, for aught I know, a count or two. They drank and smoked a great deal, talked art and music, and discussed, it seemed to me, everything that ever entered man's mind. I could only follow the general drift of what they were saying. When they discussed music it was more interesting to me; for then some fellow would run excitedly to the piano and give a demonstration of his opinions, and another would follow quickly doing the same. In this way, I learned that, regardless of what his specialty might be, every man in the party was a musician. I was at the same time impressed with the falsity of the general idea that Frenchmen are excitable and emotional, and that Germans are calm and phlegmatic. Frenchmen are merely gay and never overwhelmed by their emotions. When they talk loud and fast it is merely talk, while Germans get worked up and red in the face when sustaining an opinion; and in heated discussions are likely to allow their emotions to sweep them off their feet.

My "millionaire" planned, in the midst of the discussion on music, to have me play the "new American music" and astonish everybody present. The result was that I was more astonished than anyone else. I went to the piano and played the most intricate ragtime piece I knew. Before there was time for anybody to express an opinion on what I had done, a big be-spectacled, bushy-headed man rushed over, and, shoving me out of the chair, exclaimed, "Get up! Get up!" He seated himself at the piano, and taking the theme of my ragtime, played it through first in straight chords; then varied and developed it through every known musical form. I sat amazed. I had been turning classic music into ragtime, a comparatively easy task; and this man had taken ragtime and made it classic. The thought came across me like a flash.—It can be done, why can't I do it? From that moment my mind was made up. I clearly saw the way of carrying out the ambition I had formed when a boy.

I now lost interest in our trip. I thought, here I am a man, no longer a boy, and what am I doing but wasting my time and abusing my talent. What use am I making of my gifts? What future have I before me following my present course? These thoughts made me feel remorseful, and put me in a fever to get to work, to begin to do something. Of course I know now that I was not wasting time; that there was nothing I could have done at that age which would have benefited me more than going to Europe as I did. The desire to begin work grew stronger each day. I could think of nothing else. I made up my mind to go back into the very heart of the South, to live among the people, and drink in my inspiration first-hand. I gloated over the immense amount of material I had to work with, not only modern ragtime, but also the old slave songs,—material which no one had yet touched.

The more decided and anxious I became to return to the United States, the more I dreaded the ordeal of breaking with my "millionaire." Between this peculiar man and me there had grown a very strong bond of affection, backed up by a debt which each owed to the other. He had taken me from a terrible life in New York and by giving me the opportunity of traveling and of coming in contact with the people with whom he associated, had made me a polished man of the world. On the other hand, I was his chief means of disposing of the thing which seemed to sum up all in life that he dreaded—Time. As I remember him now, I can see that time was what he was always endeavoring to escape, to bridge over, to blot out; and it is not strange that some years later he did escape it forever, by leaping into eternity.

For some weeks I waited for just the right moment in which to tell my patron of my decision. Those weeks were a trying time to me. I felt that I was playing the part of a traitor to my best friend. At length, one day, he said to me, "Well, get ready for a long trip; we are going to Egypt, and then to Japan." The temptation was for an instant almost overwhelming, but I summoned determination enough to say, "I don't think I want to go." "What!" he exclaimed, "you want to go back to your dear Paris? You still think that the only spot on earth? Wait until you see Cairo and Tokio, you may change your mind." "No," I stammered, "it is not because I want to go back to Paris. I want to go back to the United States." He wished to know my reason, and I told him, as best I could, my dreams, my ambition, and my decision. While I was talking he watched me with a curious, almost cynical, smile growing on his lips. When I had finished he put his hand on my shoulder.—This was the first physical expression of tender regard he had ever shown me—and looking at me in a big-brotherly way, said, "My boy, you are by blood, by appearance, by education and by tastes, a white man. Now why do you want to throw your life away amidst the poverty and ignorance, in the hopeless struggle of the black people of the United States? Then look at the terrible handicap you are placing on yourself by going home and working as a Negro composer; you can never he able to get the hearing for your work which it might deserve. I doubt that even a white musician of recognized ability could succeed there by working on the theory that American music should be based on Negro themes. Music is a universal art; anybody's music belongs to everybody; you can't limit it to race or country. Now, if you want to become a composer, why not stay right here in Europe? I will put you under the best teachers on the continent. Then if you want to write music on Negro themes, why, go ahead and do it."

We talked for some time on music and the race question. On the latter subject I had never before heard him express any opinion. Between him and me no suggestion of racial differences had ever come up. I found that he was a man entirely free from prejudice, but he recognized that prejudice was a big stubborn entity which had to be taken into account. He went on to say, "This idea you have of making a Negro out of yourself is nothing more than a sentiment; and you do not realize the fearful import of what you intend to do. What kind of a Negro would you make now, especially in the South? If you had remained there, or perhaps even in your club in New York, you might have succeeded very well; but now you would be miserable. I can imagine no more dissatisfied human being than an educated, cultured and refined colored man in the United States. I have given more study to the race question in the United States than you may suppose, and I sympathize with the Negroes there; but what's the use? I can't right their wrongs, and neither can you; they must do that themselves. They are unfortunate in having wrongs to right, and you would be foolish to unnecessarily take their wrongs on your shoulders. Perhaps some day, through study and observation, you will come to see that evil is a force and, like the physical and chemical forces, we cannot annihilate it; we may only change its form. We light upon one evil and hit it with all the might of our civilization, but only succeed in scattering it into a dozen of other forms. We hit slavery through a great civil war. Did we destroy it? No, we only changed it into hatred between sections of the country: in the South, into political corruption and chicanery, the degradation of the blacks through peonage, unjust laws, unfair and cruel treatment; and the degradation of the whites by their resorting to these practices; the paralyzation of the public conscience, and the ever overhanging dread of what the future may bring. Modern civilization hit ignorance of the masses through the means of popular education. What has it done but turn ignorance into anarchy, socialism, strikes, hatred between poor and rich, and universal discontent. In like manner, modern philanthropy hit at suffering and disease through asylums and hospitals; it prolongs the sufferers' lives, it is true; but is, at the same time, sending down strains of insanity and weakness into future generations. My philosophy of life is this: make yourself as happy as possible, and try to make those happy whose lives come into touch with yours; but to attempt to right the wrongs and ease the sufferings of the world in general, is a waste of effort. You had just as well try to bale the Atlantic by pouring the water into the Pacific."

This tremendous flow of serious talk from a man I was accustomed to see either gay or taciturn so surprised and overwhelmed me that I could not frame a reply. He left me thinking over what he had said. Whatever was the soundness of his logic or the moral tone of his philosophy, his argument greatly impressed me. I could see, in spite of the absolute selfishness upon which it was based, that there was reason and common sense in it. I began to analyze my own motives, and found that they, too, were very largely mixed with selfishness. Was it more a desire to help those I considered my people or more a desire to distinguish myself, which was leading me back to the United States? That is a question I have never definitely answered.

For several weeks longer I was in a troubled state of mind. Added to the fact that I was loath to leave my good friend, was the weight of the question he had aroused in my mind, whether I was not making a fatal mistake. I suffered more than one sleepless night during that time. Finally, I settled the question on purely selfish grounds, in accordance with my "millionaire's" philosophy. I argued that music offered me a better future than anything else I had any knowledge of, and, in opposition to my friend's opinion, that I should have greater chances of attracting attention as a colored composer than as a white one. But I must own that I also felt stirred by an unselfish desire to voice all the joys and sorrows, the hopes and ambitions, of the American Negro, in classic musical form.

When my mind was fully made up I told my friend. He asked me when I intended to start. I replied that I would do so at once. He then asked me how much money I had. I told him that I had saved several hundred dollars out of sums he had given me. He gave me a check for $500, told me to write to him care of his Paris hankers if I ever needed his help, wished me good luck, and bade me good-by. All this he did almost coldly; and I often wondered whether he was in a hurry to get rid of what he considered a fool, or whether he was striving to hide deeper feelings of sorrow.

And so I separated from the man who was, all in all, the best friend I ever had, except my mother, the man who exerted the greatest influence ever brought into my life, except that exerted by my mother. My affection for him was so strong, my recollections of him are so distinct; he was such a peculiar and striking character, that I could easily fill several chapters with reminiscences of him; but for fear of tiring the reader I shall go on with my narration.

I decided to go to Liverpool and take ship for Boston. I still had an uneasy feeling about returning to New York; and in a few days I found myself aboard ship headed for home.

CHAPTER X

Among the first of my fellow passengers of whom I took any particular notice, was a tall, broad-shouldered, almost gigantic, colored man. His dark-brown face was clean shaven; he was well dressed and bore a decidedly distinguished air. In fact, if he was not handsome, he at least compelled admiration for his fine physical proportions. He attracted general attention as he strode the deck in a sort of majestic loneliness. I became curious to know who he was and determined to strike up an acquaintance with him at the first opportune moment. The chance came a day or two later. He was sitting in the smoking-room, with a cigar in his mouth which had gone out, reading a novel. I sat down beside him and, offering him a fresh cigar, said, "You don't mind my telling you something unpleasant, do you?" He looked at me with a smile, accepted the proffered cigar, and replied in a voice which comported perfectly with his size and appearance, "I think my curiosity overcomes any objections I might have." "Well," I said, "have you noticed that the man who sat at your right in the saloon during the first meal has not sat there since?" He frowned slightly without answering my question. "Well," I continued, "he asked the steward to remove him; and not only that, he attempted to persuade a number of the passengers to protest against your presence in the dining-saloon." The big man at my side took a long draw from his cigar, threw his head back and slowly blew a great cloud of smoke toward the ceiling. Then turning to me he said, "Do you know, I don't object to anyone having prejudices so long as those prejudices don't interfere with my personal liberty. Now, the man you are speaking of had a perfect right to change his seat if I in any way interfered with his appetite or his digestion. I would have no reason to complain if he removed to the farthest corner of the saloon, or even if he got off the ship; but when his prejudice attempts to move me one foot, one inch, out of the place where I am comfortably located, then I object." On the word "object" he brought his great fist down on the table in front of us with such a crash that everyone in the room turned to look. We both covered up the slight embarrassment with a laugh, and strolled out on the deck.

We walked the deck for an hour or more, discussing different phases of the Negro question. I, in referring to the race, used the personal pronoun "we"; my companion made no comment about it, nor evinced any surprise, except to slightly raise his eyebrows the first time he caught the significance of the word. He was the broadest minded colored man I have ever talked with on the Negro question. He even went so far as to sympathize with and offer excuses for some white Southern points of view. I asked him what were his main reasons for being so hopeful. He replied, "In spite of all that is written, said and done, this great, big, incontrovertible fact stands out,—the Negro is progressing, and that disproves all the arguments in the world that he is incapable of progress. I was born in slavery, and at emancipation was set adrift a ragged, penniless bit of humanity. I have seen the Negro in every grade, and I know what I am talking about. Our detractors point to the increase of crime as evidence against us; certainly we have progressed in crime as in other things; what less could be expected? And yet, in this respect, we are far from the point which has been reached by the more highly civilized white race. As we continue to progress, crime among us will gradually lose much of its brutal, vulgar, I might say healthy, aspect, and become more delicate, refined and subtile. Then it will be less shocking and noticeable, although more dangerous to society." Then dropping his tone of irony, he continued with some show of eloquence, "But, above all, when I am discouraged and disheartened, I have this to fall back on: if there is a principle of right in the world, which finally prevails, and I believe that there is if there is a merciful but justice-loving God in heaven, and I believe that there is, we shall win; for we have right on our side; while those who oppose us can defend themselves by nothing in the moral law, nor even by anything in the enlightened thought of the present age."

For several days, together with other topics, we discussed the race problem, not only of the United States, but the race problem as it affected native Africans and Jews. Finally, before we reached Boston, our conversation had grown familiar and personal. I had told him something of my past and much about my intentions for the future. I learned that he was a physician, a graduate of Howard University, Washington, and had done post-graduate work in Philadelphia; and this was his second trip abroad to attend professional courses. He had practiced for some years in the city of Washington, and though he did not say so, I gathered that his practice was a lucrative one. Before we left the ship he had made me promise that I would stop two or three days in Washington before going on South.

We put up at a hotel in Boston for a couple of days, and visited several of my new friend's acquaintances; they were all people of education and culture and, apparently, of means. I could not but help being struck by the great difference between them and the same class of colored people in the South. In speech and thought they were genuine Yankees. The difference was especially noticeable in their speech. There was none of that heavy-tongued enunciation which characterizes even the best educated colored people of the South. It is remarkable, after all, what an adaptable creature the Negro is. I have seen the black West India gentleman in London, and he is in speech and manners a perfect Englishman. I have seen natives of Haiti and Martinique in Paris, and they are more Frenchy than a Frenchman. I have no doubt that the Negro would make a good Chinaman, with exception of the pigtail.

My stay in Washington, instead of being two or three days, was two or three weeks. This was my first visit to the National Capital, and I was, of course, interested in seeing the public buildings and something of the working of the government; but most of my time I spent with the doctor among his friends and acquaintances. The social phase of life among colored people, which I spoke of in an earlier chapter, is more developed in Washington than in any other city in the country. This is on account of the large number of individuals earning good salaries and having a reasonable amount of leisure time to be drawn from. There are dozens of physicians and lawyers, scores of school teachers and hundreds of clerks in the departments. As to the colored department clerks, I think it fair to say that in educational equipment they average above the white clerks of the same grade; for, whereas a colored college graduate will seek such a job, the white university man goes into one of the many higher vocations which are open to him.

In a previous chapter I spoke of social life among colored people; so there is no need to take it up again here. But there is one thing I did not mention: among Negroes themselves there is the peculiar inconsistency of a color question. Its existence is rarely admitted and hardly ever mentioned; it may not be too strong a statement to say that the greater portion of the race is unconscious of its influence; yet this influence, though silent, is constant. It is evidenced most plainly in marriage selection; thus the black men generally marry women fairer than themselves; while, on the other hand, the dark women of stronger mental endowment are very often married to light-complexioned men; the effect is a tendency toward lighter complexions, especially among the more active elements in the race. Some might claim that this is a tacit admission of colored people among themselves of their own inferiority judged by the color line. I do not think so. What I have termed an inconsistency is, after all, most natural; it is, in fact, a tendency in accordance with what might be called an economic necessity. So far as racial differences go, the United States puts a greater premium on color, or better, lack of color, than upon anything else in the world. To paraphrase, "Have a white skin, and all things else may be added unto you." I have seen advertisements in newspapers for waiters, bell boys or elevator men, which read, "Light colored man wanted." It is this tremendous pressure which the sentiment of the country exerts that is operating on the race. There is involved not only the question of higher opportunity, but often the question of earning a livelihood; and so I say it is not strange, but a natural tendency. Nor is it any more a sacrifice of self respect that a black man should give to his children every advantage he can which complexion of the skin carries, than that the new or vulgar rich should purchase for their children the advantages which ancestry, aristocracy, and social position carry. I once heard a colored man sum it up in these words, "It's no disgrace to be black, but it's often very inconvenient."

Washington shows the Negro not only at his best, but also at his worst. As I drove around with the doctor, he commented rather harshly on those of the latter class which we saw. He remarked: "You see those lazy, loafing, good-for-nothing darkies, they're not worth digging graves for; yet they are the ones who create impressions of the race for the casual observer. It's because they are always in evidence on the street corners, while the rest of us are hard at work, and you know a dozen loafing darkies make a bigger crowd and a worse impression in this country than fifty white men of the same class. But they ought not to represent the race. We are the race, and the race ought to be judged by us, not by them. Every race and every nation is judged by the best it has been able to produce, not by the worst."

The recollection of my stay in Washington is a pleasure to me now. In company with the doctor I visited Howard University, the public schools, the excellent colored hospital, with which he was in some way connected, if I remember correctly, and many comfortable and even elegant homes. It was with some reluctance that I continued my journey south. The doctor was very kind in giving me letters to people in Richmond and Nashville when I told him that I intended to stop in both of these cities. In Richmond a man who was then editing a very creditable colored newspaper, gave nie a great deal of his time, and made my stay there of three or four days very pleasant. In Nashville I spent a whole day at Fisk University, the home of the "Jubilee Singers," and was more than repaid for my time. Among my letters of introduction was one to a very prosperous physician, He drove me about the city and introduced me to a number of people. From Nashville I went to Atlanta, where I stayed long enough to gratify an old desire to see Atlanta University again. I then continued my journey to Macon.

During the trip from Nashville to Atlanta I went into the smoking compartment of the car to smoke a cigar. I was traveling in a Pullman, not because of an abundance of funds, but because through my experience with my "millionaire," a certain amount of comfort and luxury had become a necessity to me whenever it was obtainable. When I entered the car I found only a couple of men there; but in a half hour there were half a dozen or more. From the general conversation I learned that a fat Jewish looking man was a cigar manufacturer, and was experimenting in growing Havana tobacco in Florida; that a slender be-spectacled young man was from Ohio and a professor in some State institution in Alabama; that a white-mustached, well dressed man was an old Union soldier who had fought through the Civil War; and that a tall, raw-boned, red-faced man, who seemed bent on leaving nobody in ignorance of the fact that he was from Texas, was a cotton planter.

In the North men may ride together for hours in a "smoker" and unless they are acquainted with each other never exchange a word; in the South, men thrown together in such manner are friends in fifteen minutes. There is always present a warm-hearted cordiality which will melt down the most frigid reserve. It may be because Southerners are very much like Frenchmen in that they must talk; and not only must they talk, but they must express their opinions.

The talk in the car was for a while miscellaneous,—on the weather, crops, business prospects—the old Union soldier had invested capital in Atlanta, and he predicted that that city would soon be one of the greatest in the country—finally the conversation drifted to politics; then, as a natural sequence, turned upon the Negro question.

In the discussion of the race question, the diplomacy of the Jew was something to he admired; he had the faculty of agreeing with everybody without losing his allegiance to any side. He knew that to sanction Negro oppression would be to sanction Jewish oppression, and would expose him to a shot along that line from the old soldier, who stood firmly on the ground of equal rights and opportunity to all men; yet long traditions and business instincts told him, when in Rome to act as a Roman. Altogether his position was a delicate one, and I gave him credit for the skill he displayed in maintaining it. The young professor was apologetic. He had had the same views as the G.A.R. man; but a year in the South had opened his eyes, and he had to confess that the problem could hardly be handled any better than it was being handled by the Southern whites. To which the G.A.R. man responded somewhat rudely that he had spent ten times as many years in the South as his young friend, and that he could easily understand how holding a position in a State institution in Alabama would bring about a change of views. The professor turned very red and had very little more to say. The Texan was fierce, eloquent and profane in his argument and, in a lower sense, there was a direct logic in what he said, which was convincing; it was only by taking higher ground, by dealing in what Southerners call "theories" that he could be combatted. Occasionally some one of the several other men in the "smoker" would throw in a remark to reinforce what he said, but he really didn't need any help; he was sufficient in himself.

In the course of a short time the controversy narrowed itself down to an argument between the old soldier and the Texan. The latter maintained hotly that the Civil War was a criminal mistake on the part of the North, and that the humiliation which the South suffered during Reconstruction could never be forgotten. The Union man retorted just as hotly that the South was responsible for the war, and that the spirit of unforgetfulness on its part was the greatest cause of present friction; that it seemed to be the one great aim of the South to convince the North that the latter made a mistake in fighting to preserve the Union and liberate the slaves. "Can you imagine," he went on to say, "what would have been the condition of things eventually if there had been no war, and the South had been allowed to follow its course? Instead of one great, prosperous country with nothing before it but the conquests of peace, a score of petty republics, as in Central and South America, wasting their energies in war with each other or in revolutions."

"Well," replied the Texan, "anything—no country at all is better than having niggers over you. But anyhow, the war was fought and the niggers were freed; for it's no use beating around the bush, the niggers, and not the Union, was the cause of it; and now do you believe that all the niggers on earth are worth the good white blood that was spilt? You freed the nigger and you gave him the ballot, but you couldn't make a citizen out of him. He don't know what he's voting for, and we buy 'em like so many hogs. You're giving 'em education, but that only makes slick rascals out of 'em."

"Don't fancy for a moment," said the Northern man, "that you have any monopoly in buying ignorant votes. The same thing is done on a larger scale in New York and Boston, and in Chicago and San Francisco; and they are not black votes either. As to education making the Negro worse, you had just as well tell me that religion does the same thing. And, by the way, how many educated colored men do you know personally?"

The Texan admitted that he knew only one, and added that he was in the penitentiary. "But," he said, "do you mean to claim, ballot or no ballot, education or no education, that niggers are the equals of white men?"

"That's not the question," answered the other, "but if the Negro is so distinctly inferior, it is a strange thing to me that it takes such tremendous effort on the part of the white man to make him realize it, and to keep him in the same place into which inferior men naturally fall. However, let us grant for sake of argument that the Negro is inferior in every respect to the white man; that fact only increases our moral responsibility in regard to our actions toward him. Inequalities of numbers, wealth and power, even of intelligence and morals, should make no difference in the essential rights of men."

"If he's inferior and weaker, and is shoved to the wall, that's his own look out," said the Texan. "That's the law of nature; and he's bound to go to the wall; for no race in the world has ever been able to stand competition with the Anglo-Saxon. The Anglo-Saxon race has always been and always will be the masters of the world, and the niggers in the South ain't going to change all the records of history."

"My friend," said the old soldier slowly, "if you have studied history, will you tell me, as confidentially between white men, what the Anglo-Saxon has ever done?"

The Texan was too much astonished by the question to venture any reply.

His opponent continued, "Can you name a single one of the great fundamental and original intellectual achievements which have raised man in the scale of civilization that may be credited to the Anglo-Saxon? The art of letters, of poetry, of music, of sculpture, of painting, of the drama, of architecture; the science of mathematics, of astronomy, of philosophy, of logic, of physics, of chemistry, the use of the metals and the principles of mechanics, were all invented or discovered by darker and what we now call inferior races and nations. We have carried many of these to their highest point of perfection, but the foundation was laid by others. D'o you know the only original contribution to civilization we can claim is what we have done in steam and electricity and in making implements of war more deadly; and there we worked largely on principles which we did not discover. Why, we didn't even originate the religion we use. We are a great race, the greatest in the world to-day, but we ought to remember that we are standing on a pile of past races, and enjoy our position with a little less show of arrogance. We are simply having our turn at the game, and we were a long time getting to it. After all, racial supremacy is merely a matter of dates in history. The man here who belongs to what is, all in all, the greatest race the world ever produced, is almost ashamed to own it. If the Anglo-Saxon is the source of everything good and great in the human race from the beginning, why wasn't the German forest the birthplace of civilization?"

The Texan was somewhat disconcerted, for the argument had passed a little beyond his limits, but he swung it back to where he was sure of his ground by saying, "All that may be true, but it hasn't got much to do with us and the niggers here in the South. We've got 'em here, and we've got 'em to live with, and it's a question of white man or nigger, no middle ground. You want us to treat niggers as equals. Do you want to see 'em sitting around in our parlors? Do you want to see a mulatto South? To bring it right home to you, would you let your daughter marry a nigger?"

"No, I wouldn't consent to my daughter's marrying a nigger, but that doesn't prevent my treating a black man fairly. And I don't see what fair treatment has to do with niggers sitting around in your parlors; they can't come there unless they're invited. Out of all the white men I know, only a hundred or so have the privilege of sitting around in my parlor. As to the mulatto South, if you Southerners have one boast that is stronger than another, it is your women; you put them on a pinnacle of purity and virtue and bow down in a chivalric worship before them; yet you talk and act as though, should you treat the Negro fairly and take the anti-intermarriage laws off your statute books, these same women would rush into the arms of black lovers and husbands. It's a wonder to me that they don't rise up and resent the insult."

"Colonel," said the Texan, as he reached into his handbag and brought out a large flask of whiskey, "you might argue from now until hell freezes over, and you might convince me that you're right, but you'll never convince me that I'm wrong. All you say sounds very good, but it's got nothing to do with facts. You can say what men ought to be, but they ain't that; so there you are. Down here in the South we're up against facts, and we're meeting 'em like facts. We don't believe the nigger is or ever will be the equal of the white man, and we ain't going to treat him as an equal; I'll be damned if we will. Have a drink." Everybody, except the professor, partook of the generous Texan's flask, and the argument closed in a general laugh and good feeling.

I went back into the main part of the car with the conversation on my mind. Here I had before me the bald, raw, naked aspects of the race question in the South; and, in consideration of the step I was just taking, it was far from encouraging. The sentiments of the Texan—and he expressed the sentiments of the South—fell upon me like a chill. I was sick at heart. Yet, I must confess that underneath it all I felt a certain sort of admiration for the man who could not be swayed from what he held as his principles. Contrasted with him, the young Ohio professor was indeed a pitiable character. And all along, in spite of myself, I have been compelled to accord the same kind of admiration to the Southern white man for the manner in which he defends not only his virtues but his vices. He knows, that judged by a high standard, he is narrow and prejudiced, that he is guilty of unfairness, oppression and cruelty, but this he defends as stoutly as he would his better qualities. This same spirit obtains in a great degree among the blacks; they, too, defend their faults and failings. This spirit carries them so far at times as to make them sympathizers with members of their race who are perpetrators of crime. And, yet,

among themselves they are their own most merciless critics. I have never
heard the race so terribly arraigned as I have by colored speakers to
strictly colored audiences. It is the spirit of the South to defend everything
belonging to it. The North is too cosmopolitan and tolerant for such a
spirit. If you should say to an Easterner that Paris is a gayer city than
New York he would be likely to agree with you, or at least to let you have
your way; but to suggest to a South Carolinian that Boston is a nicer city
to live in than Charleston would be to stir his greatest depths of argument
and eloquence.

But, to-day, as I think over that smoking-car argument, I can see it in
a different light. The Texan's position does not render things so hopeless,
for it indicates that the main difficulty of the race question does not lie so
much in the actual condition of the blacks as it does in the mental attitude
of the whites; and a mental attitude, especially one not based on truth,
can be changed more easily than actual conditions. That is to say, the
burden of the question is not that the whites are struggling to save ten
million despondent and moribund people from sinking into a hopeless
slough of ignorance, poverty and barbarity in their very midst, but that
they are unwilling to open certain doors of opportunity and to accord
certain treatment to ten million aspiring,
education~and~property-acquiring people. In a word, the difficulty of the
problem is not so much due to the facts presented, as to the hypothesis
assumed for its solution. In this it is similar to the problem of the Solar
System. By a complex, confusing and almost contradictory mathematical
process, by the use of zigzags instead of straight lines, the earth can be
proven to be the center of things celestial; but by an operation so simple
that it can be comprehended by a schoolboy, its position can be verified
among the other worlds which revolve about the sun, and its movements
harmonized with the laws of the universe. So, when the white race
assumes as a hypothesis that it is the main object of creation, and that all
things else are merely subsidiary to its well being, sophism, subterfuge,
perversion of conscience, arrogance, injustice, oppression, cruelty, sacrifice
of human blood, all are required to maintain the position, and its dealings
with other races become indeed a problem, a problem which, if based on
a hypothesis of common humanity, could be solved by the simple rules of
justice.

When I reached Macon I decided to leave my trunk and all my surplus
belongings, to pack my bag, and strike out into the interior. This I did;
and by train, by mule and ox-cart, I traveled through many counties. This
was my first real experience among rural colored people, and all that I
saw was interesting to me; but there was a great deal which does not
require description at my hands; for log cabins and plantations and
dialect-speaking darkies are perhaps better known in American literature
than any other single picture of our national life. Indeed, they form an
ideal and exclusive literary concept of the American Negro to such an
extent that it is almost impossible to get the reading public to recognize
him in any other setting; but I shall endeavor to avoid giving the reader
any already overworked and hackneyed descriptions. This generally

accepted literary ideal of the American Negro constitutes what is really an obstacle in the way of the thoughtful and progressive element of the race. His character has been established as a happy-go-lucky, laughing, shuffling, banjo-picking being, and the reading public has not yet been prevailed upon to take him seriously. His efforts to elevate himself socially are looked upon as a sort of absurd caricature of "white civilization." A novel dealing with colored people who lived in respectable homes and amidst a fair degree of culture and who naturally acted "just like white folks" would be taken in a comic opera sense. In this respect the Negro is much in the position of a great comedian who gives up the lighter rôles to play tragedy. No matter how well he may portray the deeper passions, the public is loth to give him up in his old character; they even conspire to make him a failure in serious work, in order to force him back into comedy. In the same respect, the public is not too much to be blamed, for great comedians are far more scarce than mediocre tragedians; every amateur actor is a tragedian. However, this very fact constitutes the opportunity of the future Negro novelist and poet to give the country something new and unknown, in depicting the life, the ambitions, the struggles and the passions of those of their race who are striving to break the narrow limits of traditions. A beginning has already been made in that remarkable book by Dr. Du Bois, "The Souls of Black Folk."

Much, too, that I saw while on this trip, in spite of my enthusiasm, was disheartening. Often I thought of what my "millionaire" had said to me, and wished myself back in Europe. The houses in which I had to stay were generally uncomfortable, sometimes worse. I often had to sleep in a division or compartment with several other people. Once or twice I was not so fortunate as to find divisions; everybody slept on pallets on the floor. Frequently I was able to lie down and contemplate the stars which were in their zenith. The food was at times so distasteful and poorly cooked that I could not eat it. I remember that once I lived for a week or more on buttermilk, on account of not being able to stomach the fat bacon, the rank turnip tops and the heavy damp mixture of meal, salt and water, which was called corn bread. It was only my ambition to do the work which I had planned that kept me steadfast to my purpose. Occasionally I would meet with some signs of progress and uplift in even one of these backwood settlements—houses built of boards, with windows, and divided into rooms, decent food and a fair standard of living. This condition was due to the fact that there was in the community some exceptionally capable Negro farmer whose thrift served as an example. As I went about among these dull, simple people, the great majority of them hard working; in their relations with the whites, submissive, faithful, and often affectionate, negatively content with their lot, and contrasted them with those of the race who had been quickened by the forces of thought, I could not but appreciate the logic of the position held by those Southern leaders who have been bold enough to proclaim against the education of the Negro. They are consistent in their public speech with Southern sentiment and desires. Those public men of the South who have not been daring or heedless enough to defy the ideals of twentieth century civilization and of modern humanitarianism and philanthropy, find themselves in the embarrassing situation of preaching one thing and praying for another. They are in the position of the fashionable woman who is compelled by the laws of polite society to say to her dearest enemy, "How happy I am to see you."

And yet in this respect how perplexing is Southern character; for in opposition to the above, it may be said that the claim of the Southern whites that they love the Negro better than the Northern whites do, is in a manner true. Northern white people love the Negro in a sort of abstract way, as a race; through a sense of justice, charity and philanthropy, they will liberally assist in his elevation. A number of them have heroically spent their lives in this effort (and just here I wish to say that when the colored people reach the monument building stage, they should not forget the men and women who went South after the war and founded schools for them). Yet, generally speaking, they have no particular liking for individuals of the race. Southern white people despise the Negro as a race, and will do nothing to aid in his elevation as such; but for certain individuals they have a strong affection, and are helpful to them in many ways. With these individual members of the race they live on terms of the greatest intimacy; they intrust to them their children, their family treasures and their family secrets; in trouble they often go to them for comfort and counsel; in sickness they often rely upon their care. This affectionate relation between the Southern whites and those blacks who come into close touch with them has not been overdrawn even in fiction.

This perplexity of Southern character extends even to the mixture of the races. That is spoken of as though it were dreaded worse than smallpox, leprosy or the plague. Yet, when I was in Jacksonville I knew several prominent families there with large colored branches, which went by the same name and were known and acknowledged as blood relatives. And what is more, there seemed to exist between these black brothers and sisters and uncles and aunts a decided friendly feeling.

I said above that Southern whites would do nothing for the Negro as a race. I know the South claims that it has spent millions for the education of the blacks, and that it has of its own free will shouldered this awful burden. It seems to be forgetful of the fact that these millions have been taken from the public tax funds for education, and that the law of political economy which recognizes the land owner as the one who really pays the taxes is not tenable. It would be just as reasonable for the relatively few land-owners of Manhattan to complain that they had to stand the financial burden of the education of the thousands and thousands of children whose parents pay rent for tenements and flats. Let the millions of producing and consuming Negroes be taken out of the South, and it would be quickly seen how much less of public funds there would be to appropriate for education or any other purpose.

In thus traveling about through the country, I was sometimes amused on arriving at some little railroad-station town to be taken for and treated as a white man, and six hours later, when it was learned that I was stopping at the house of the colored preacher or school teacher, to note the attitude of the whole town change. At times this led even to embarrassment. Yet it cannot be so embarrassing for a colored man to be taken for white as for a white man to be taken for colored; and I have heard of several cases of the latter kind.

All this while I was gathering material for work, jotting down in my note-book themes and melodies, and trying to catch the spirit of the Negro in his relatively primitive state. I began to feel the necessity of hurrying so that I might get back to some city like Nashville to begin my compositions, and at the same time earn at least a living by teaching and performing before my funds gave out. At the last settlement in which I stopped I found a mine of material. This was due to the fact that "big meeting" was in progress. "Big meeting" is an institution something like camp-meeting; the difference being that it is held in a permanent church, and not in a temporary structure. All the churches of some one denomination—of course, either Methodist or Baptist—in a county or, perhaps, in several adjoining counties, are closed, and the congregations unite at some centrally located church for a series of meetings lasting a week. It is really a social as well as a religious function. The people come in great numbers, making the trip, according to their financial status, in buggies drawn by sleek, fleet-footed mules, in ox-teams, or on foot. It was amusing to see some of the latter class trudging down the hot and dusty road with their shoes, which were brand new, strung across their shoulders. When they got near the church they sat on the side of the road and, with many grimaces, tenderly packed their feet into those instruments of torture. This furnished, indeed, a trying test of their religion. The famous preachers come from near and far, and take turns in warning sinners of the day of wrath. Food, in the form of those two Southern luxuries, fried chicken and roast pork, is plentiful, and no one need go hungry. On the opening Sunday the women are immaculate in starched stiff white dresses adorned with ribbons either red or blue. Even a great many of the men wear streamers of van-colored ribbons in the button-holes of their coats. A few of them carefully cultivate a fore lock of hair by wrapping it in twine, and on such festive occasions decorate it with a narrow ribbon streamer. Big meetings afford a fine opportunity to the younger people to meet each other dressed in their Sunday clothes, and much rustic courting, which is as enjoyable as any other kind, is indulged in.

This big meeting which I was lucky enough to catch was particularly well attended; the extra large attendance was due principally to two attractions, a man by name of John Brown, who was renowned as the most powerful preacher for miles around; and a wonderful leader of singing, who was known as "Singing Johnson." These two men were a study and a revelation to me. They caused me to reflect upon how great an influence their types have been in the development of the Negro in America. Both these types are now looked upon generally with condescension or contempt by the progressive element among the colored people; but it should never be forgotten that it was they who led/the race from paganism, and kept it steadfast to Christianity through all the long, dark years of slavery.

John Brown was a jet black man of medium size, with a strikingly intelligent head and face, and a voice like an organ peal. He preached each night after several lesser lights successively held the pulpit during an hour or so. As far as subject matter is concerned, all of the sermons were alike; each began with the fall of man, ran through various trials and tribulations of the Hebrew children, on to the redemption by Christ, and ended with a fervid picture of the judgment day and the fate of the damned. But John Brown possessed magnetism and an imagination so free and daring that he was able to carry through what the other preachers would not attempt. He knew all the arts and tricks of oratory, the modulation of the voice to almost a whisper, the pause for effect, the rise through light, rapid fire sentences to the terrific, thundering outburst of an electrifying climax. In addition, he had the intuition of a born theatrical manager. Night after night this man held me fascinated. He convinced me that, after all, eloquence consists more in the manner of saying than in what is said. It is largely a matter of tone pictures.

The most striking example of John Brown's magnetism and imagination was his "heavenly march"; I shall never forget how it impressed me when I heard it. He opened his sermon in the usual way; then proclaiming to his listeners that he was going to take them on the heavenly march, he seized the Bible under his arm and began to pace up and down the pulpit platform. The congregation immediately began with their feet a tramp, tramp, tramp, in time with the preacher's march in the pulpit, all the while singing in an undertone a hymn about marching to Zion. Suddenly he cried, "Halt!" Every foot stopped with the precision of a company of well drilled soldiers, and the singing ceased. The morning star had been reached. Here the preacher described the beauties of that celestial body. Then the march, the tramp, tramp, tramp, and the singing was again taken up. Another "Halt!" They had reached the evening star. And so on, past the sun and the moon—the intensity of religious emotion all the time increasing—along the milky way, on up to the gates of heaven. Here the halt was longer, and the preacher described at length the gates and walls of the New Jerusalem. Then he took his hearers through the pearly gates, along the golden streets, pointing out the glories of the City, pausing occasionally to greet some patriarchal members of the church, well known to most of his listeners in life, who had had "the tears wiped from their eyes, were clad in robes of spotless white, with crowns of gold upon their heads and harps within their hands," and ended his march before the great white throne. To the reader this may sound ridiculous, but listened to under the circumstances, it was highly and effectively dramatic. I was a more or less sophisticated and non-religious man of the world, but the torrent of the preacher's words, moving with the rhythm and glowing with the eloquence of primitive poetry swept me along, and I, too, felt like joining in the shouts of "Amen! Hallelujah!"

John Brown's powers in describing the delights of heaven were no greater than those in depicting the horrors of hell. I saw great, strapping fellows, trembling and weeping like children at the "mourners' bench." His warnings to sinners were truly terrible. I shall never forget one expression that he used, which for originality and aptness could not be excelled. In my opinion, it is more graphic and, for us, far more expressive than St. Paul's "It is hard to kick against the pricks." He struck the attitude of a pugilist and thundered out, "Young man, yo' arm's too short to box wid God!"

As interesting as was John Brown to me, the other man, "Singing Johnson," was more so. He was a small, dark-brown, one-eyed man, with a clear, strong, high-pitched voice, a leader of singing, a maker of songs, a man who could improvise at the moment lines to fit the occasion. Not so striking a figure as John Brown, but, at "big meetings," equally important. It is indispensable to the success of the singing, when the congregation is a large one made up of people from different communities, to have someone with a strong voice who knows just what hymn to sing and when to sing it, who can pitch it in the right key, and who has all the leading lines committed to memory. Sometimes it devolves upon the leader to "sing down" a long-winded, or uninteresting speaker. Committing to memory the leading lines of all the Negro spiritual songs is no easy task, for they run up into the hundreds. But the accomplished leader must know them all, because the congregation sings only the refrains and repeats; every ear in the church is fixed upon him, and if he becomes mixed in his lines or forgets them, the responsibility falls directly on his shoulders.

For example, most of these hymns are constructed to be sung in the following manner:

Leader— "Swing low, sweet chariot."
Congregation—"Coming for to carry me home."
Leader— "Swing low, sweet chariot."
Congregation—"Coming for to carry me home."
Leader— "I look over yonder, what do I see?"
Congregation—"Coming for to carry me home."
Leader— "Two little angels coming after me."
Congregation—"Coming for to carry me home."
— etc., etc., etc.

The solitary and plaintive voice of the leader is answered by a sound like the roll of the sea, producing a most curious effect.

In only a few of these songs do the leader and the congregation start off together. Such a song is the well known "Steal away to Jesus."

The leader and the congregation begin:

"Steal away, steal away,
Steal away to Jesus;
Steal away, steal away home,
I ain't got long to stay here."
Then the leader alone:

"My Lord he calls me,
He calls me by the thunder,
The trumpet sounds within-a my soul."
Then all together:
"I ain't got long to stay here."

The leader and the congregation again take up the opening refrain; then the leader sings three more leading lines alone, and so on almost ad infinitum. It will be seen that even here most of the work falls upon the leader, for the congregation sings the same lines over and over, while his memory and ingenuity are taxed to keep the songs going.

Generally, the parts taken up by the congregation are sung in a three-part harmony, the women singing the soprano and a transposed tenor, the men with high voices singing the melody, and those with low voices, a thundering bass. In a few of these songs, however, the leading part is sung in unison by the whole congregation, down to the last line, which is harmonized. The effect of this is intensely thrilling. Such a hymn is "Go down Moses." It stirs the heart like a trumpet call.

"Singing Johnson" was an ideal leader; and his services were in great demand. He spent his time going about the country from one church to another. He received his support in much the same way as the preachers,—part of a collection, food and lodging. All of his leisure time he devoted to originating new words and melodies and new lines for old songs. He always sang with his eyes,—or to be more exact—his eye closed, indicating the tempo by swinging his head to and fro. He was a great judge of the proper hymn to sing at a particular moment; and I noticed several times, when the preacher reached a certain climax, or expressed a certain sentiment, that Johnson broke in with a line or two of some appropriate hymn. The speaker understood, and would pause until the singing ceased.

As I listened to the singing of these songs, the wonder of their production grew upon me more and more. How did the men who originated them manage to do it? The sentiments are easily accounted for; they are mostly taken from the Bible; but the melodies, where did they come from? Some of them so weirdly sweet, and others so wonderfully strong. Take, for instance, "Go down Moses." I doubt that there is a stronger theme in the whole musical literature of the world. And so many of these songs contain more than mere melody; there is sounded in them that elusive undertone, the note in music which is not heard with the ears. I sat often with the tears rolling down my cheeks and my heart melted within me. Any musical person who has never heard a Negro congregation under the spell of religious fervor sing these old songs, has missed one of the most thrilling emotions which the human heart may experience. Anyone who can listen to Negroes sing, "Nobody knows de trouble I see, Nobody knows but Jesus," without shedding tears, must indeed have a heart of stone.

As yet, the Negroes themselves do not fully appreciate these old slave songs. The educated classes are rather ashamed of them, and prefer to sing hymns from books. This feeling is natural; they are still too close to the conditions under which the songs were produced; but the day will come when this slave music will be the most treasured heritage of the American Negro.

At the close of the "big meeting" I left the settlement where it was being held, full of enthusiasm. I was in that frame of mind which, in the artistic temperament, amounts to inspiration. I was now ready and anxious to get to some place where I might settle down to work, and give expression the ideas which were teeming in my head; but I strayed into another deviation from my path of life as I had it marked out, which led me into an entirely different road. Instead of going to the nearest and most convenient railroad station, I accepted the invitation of a young man who had been present the closing Sunday at the meeting, to drive with him some miles farther to the town in which he taught school, and there take the train. My conversation with this young man as we drove along through the country was extremely interesting. He had been a student in one of the Negro colleges,—strange coincidence, in the very college, as I learned through him, in which "Shiny" was now a professor. I was, of course, curious to hear about my boyhood friend; and had it not been vacation time, and that I was not sure that I would find him, I should have gone out of my way to pay him a visit; but I determined to write to him as soon as the school opened. My companion talked to me about his work among the people, of his hopes and his discouragements. He was tremendously in earnest; I might say, too much so. In fact, it may be said that the majority of intelligent colored people are, in some degree, too much in earnest over the race question. They assume and carry so much that their progress is at times impeded, and they are unable to see things in their proper proportions. In many instances, a slight exercise of the sense of humor would save much anxiety of soul. Anyone who marks the general tone of editorials in colored newspapers is apt to be impressed with this idea. If the mass of Negroes took their present and future as seriously as do the most of their leaders, the race would be in no mental condition to sustain the terrible pressure which it undergoes; it would sink of its own weight. Yet, it must be acknowledged that in the making of a race over-seriousness is a far lesser failing than its reverse, and even the faults resulting from it lean toward the right.

We drove into the town just before dark. As we passed a large, unpainted church, my companion pointed it out as the place where he held his school. I promised that I would go there with him the next morning and stay a while. The town was of that kind which hardly requires or deserves description; a straggling line of brick and wooden stores on one side of the railroad track and some cottages of various sizes on the other side constituted about the whole of it. The young school teacher boarded at the best house in the place owned by a colored man. It was painted, had glass windows, contained "store bought" furniture, an organ, and lamps with chimneys. The owner held a job of some kind on the railroad. After supper it was not long before everybody was sleepy. I occupied the room with the school teacher. In a few minutes after we got into the room he was in bed and asleep; but I took advantage of the unusual luxury of a lamp which gave light, and sat looking over my notes and jotting down some ideas which were still fresh in my mind. Suddenly I became conscious of that sense of alarm which is always aroused by the sound of hurrying footsteps on the silence of the night. I stopped work, and looked at my watch. It was after eleven. I listened, straining every nerve to hear above the tumult of my quickening pulse. I caught the murmur of voices, then the gallop of a horse, then of another and another. Now thoroughly alarmed, I woke my companion, and together we both listened. After a moment he put out the light, softly opened the window-blind, and we cautiously peeped out. We saw men moving in one direction, and from the mutterings we vaguely caught the rumor that some terrible crime had been committed, murder! rape! I put on my coat and hat. My friend did all in his power to dissuade me from venturing out; but it was impossible for me to remain in the house under such tense excitement. My nerves would not have stood it. Perhaps what bravery I exercised in going out was due to the fact that I felt sure my identity as a colored man had not yet become known in the town.

I went out, and, following the drift, reached the railroad station. There was gathered there a crowd of men, all white, and others were steadily arriving, seemingly from all the surrounding country. How did the news spread so quickly? I watched these men moving under the yellow glare of the kerosene lamps about the station, stern, comparatively silent, all of them armed, some of them in boots and spurs; fierce, determined men. I had come to know the type well, blond, tall and lean, with ragged mustache and beard, and glittering gray eyes. At the first suggestion of daylight they began to disperse in groups, going in several directions. There was no extra noise or excitement, no loud talking, only swift, sharp words of command given by those who seemed to be accepted as leaders by mutual understanding. In fact, the impression made upon me was that everything was being done in quite an orderly manner. In spite of so many leaving, the crowd around the station continued to grow; at sunrise there were a great many women and children. By this time I also noticed some colored people; a few seemed to be going about customary tasks, several were standing on the outskirts of the crowd; but the gathering of Negroes usually seen in such towns was missing.

Before noon they brought him in. Two horsemen rode abreast; between them, half dragged, the poor wretch made his way through the dust. His hands were tied behind him, and ropes around his body were fastened to the saddle horns of his double guard. The men who at midnight had been stern and silent were now emitting that terror instilling sound known as the "rebel yell." A space was quickly cleared in the crowd, and a rope placed about his neck; when from somewhere came the suggestion, "Burn him!" It ran like an electric current. Have you ever witnessed the transformation of human beings into savage beasts? Nothing can be more terrible. A railroad tie was sunk into the ground, the rope was removed and a chain brought and securely coiled around the victim and the stake. There he stood, a man only in form and stature, every sign of degeneracy stamped upon his countenance. His eyes were dull and vacant, indicating not a single ray of thought. Evidently the realization of his fearful fate had robbed him of whatever reasoning power he had ever possessed. He was too stunned and stupefied even to tremble. Fuel was brought from everywhere, oil, the torch; the flames crouched for an instant as though to gather strength, then leaped up as high as their victim's head. He squirmed, he writhed, strained at his chains, then gave out cries and groans that I shall always hear. The cries and groans were choked off by the fire and smoke; but his eyes bulging from their sockets, rolled from side to side, appealing in vain for help. Some of the crowd yelled and cheered, others seemed appalled at what they had done, and there were those who turned away sickened at the sight. I was fixed to the spot where I stood, powerless to take my eyes from what I did not want to see.

It was over before I realized that time had elapsed. Before I could make myself believe that what I saw was really happening, I was looking at a scorched post, a smoldering fire, blackened hones, charred fragments sifting down through coils of chain, and the smell of burnt flesh—human flesh—was in my nostrils.

I walked a short distance away, and sat down in order to clear my dazed mind. A great wave of humiliation and shame swept over me. Shame that I belonged to a race that could be so dealt with; and shame for my country, that it, the great example of democracy to the world, should be the only civilized, if not the only state on earth, where a human being would be burned alive. My heart turned bitter within me. I could understand why Negroes are led to sympathize with even their worst criminals, and to protect them when possible. By all the impulses of normal human nature they can and should do nothing less.

Whenever I hear protests from the South that it should be left alone to deal with the Negro question, my thoughts go back to that scene of brutality and savagery. I do not see how a people that can find in its conscience any excuse whatever for slowly burning to death a human being, or to tolerate such an act, can be entrusted with the salvation of a race. Of course, there are in the South men of liberal thought who do not approve lynching; but I wonder how long they will endure the limits which are placed upon free speech. They still cower and tremble before "Southern opinion." Even so late as the recent Atlanta riot, those men who were brave enough to speak a word in behalf of justice and humanity felt called upon, by way of apology, to preface what they said with a glowing rhetorical tribute to the Anglo-Saxon's superiority, and to refer to the "great and impassable gulf" between the races "fixed by the Creator at the foundation of the world." The question of the relative qualities of the two races is still an open one. The reference to the "great gulf" loses force in face of the fact that there are in this country perhaps three or four million people with the blood of both races in their veins; but I fail to see the pertinency of either statement, subsequent to the beating and murdering of scores of innocent people in the streets of a civilized and Christian city.

The Southern whites are in many respects a great people. Looked at from a certain point of view, they are picturesque. If one will put himself in a romantic frame of mind, he can admire their notions of chivalry and bravery and justice. In this same frame of mind an intelligent man can go to the theater and applaud the impossible hero, who with his single sword slays everybody in the play except the equally impossible heroine. So can an ordinary peace-loving citizen sit by a comfortable fire and read with enjoyment of the bloody deeds of pirates and the fierce brutality of Vikings. This is the way in which we gratify the old, underlying animal instincts and passions; but we should shudder with horror at the mere idea of such practices being realities in this day of enlightened and humanitarianized thought. The Southern whites are not yet living quite in the present age; many of their general ideas hark back to a former century, some of them to the Dark Ages. In the light of other days, they are sometimes magnificent. To-day they are often ludicrous and cruel.

How long I sat with bitter thoughts running through my mind, I do not know; perhaps an hour or more. When I decided to get up and go back to the house I found that I could hardly stand on my feet. I was as weak as a man who had lost blood. However, I dragged myself along, with the central idea of a general plan well fixed in my mind. I did not find my school teacher friend at home, so did not see him again. I swallowed a few mouthfuls of food, packed my bag, and caught the afternoon train.

When I reached Macon, I stopped only long enough to get the main part of my luggage, and to buy a ticket for New York. All along the journey I was occupied in debating with myself the step which I had decided to take. I argued that to forsake one's race to better one's condition was no less worthy an action than to forsake one's country for the same purpose. I finally made up my mind that I would neither disclaim the black race nor claim the white race; but that I would change my name, raise a mustache, and let the world take me for what it would; that it was not necessary for me to go about with a label of inferiority pasted across my forehead. All the while, I understood that it was not discouragement, or fear, or search for a larger field of action and opportunity, that was driving me out of the Negro race. I knew that it was shame, unbearable shame. Shame at being identified with a people that could with impunity be treated worse than animals. For certainly the law would restrain and punish the malicious burning alive of animals.

So once again, I found myself gazing at the towers of New York, and wondering what future that city held in store for me.

CHAPTER XI

I have now reached that part of my narrative where I must be brief, and touch only lightly on important facts; therefore, the reader must make up his mind to pardon skips and jumps and meager details.

When I reached New York I was completely lost. I could not have felt more a stranger had I been suddenly dropped into Constantinople. I knew not where to turn or how to strike out. I was so oppressed by a feeling of loneliness that the temptation to visit my old home in Connecticut was well nigh irresistible. I reasoned, however, that unless I found my old music teacher, I should be, after so many years of absence, as much of a stranger there as in New York; and, furthermore, that in view of the step which I had decided to take, such a visit would be injudicious. I remembered, too, that I had some property there in the shape of a piano and a few books, but decided that it would not be worth what it might cost me to take possession.

By reason of the fact that my living expenses in the South had been very small, I still had nearly four hundred dollars of my capital left. In contemplation of this, my natural and acquired Bohemian tastes asserted themselves, and I decided to have a couple of weeks' good time before worrying seriously about the future. I went to Coney Island and the other resorts; took in the pre-season shows along Broadway, and ate at first class restaurants; but I shunned the old Sixth Avenue district as though it were pest infected. My few days of pleasure made appalling inroads upon what cash I had, and caused me to see that it required a good deal of money to live in New York as I wished to live, and that I should have to find, very soon, some more or less profitable employment. I was sure that unknown, without friends or prestige, it would be useless to try to establish myself as a teacher of music; so I gave that means of earning a livelihood scarcely any consideration. And even had I considered it possible to secure pupils, as I then felt, I should have hesitated about taking up a work in which the chances for any considerable financial success are necessarily so small. I had made up my mind that since I was not going to be a Negro, I would avail myself of every possible opportunity to make a white man's success; and that, if it can be summed up in any one word, means "money."

I watched the "want" columns in the newspapers and answered a number of advertisements; but in each case found the positions were such as I could not fill or did not want. I also spent several dollars for "ads" which brought me no replies. In this way I came to know the hopes and disappointments of a large and pitiable class of humanity in this great city, the people who look for work through the newspapers. After some days of this sort of experience, I concluded that the main difficulty with me was that I was not prepared for what I wanted to do. I then decided upon a course which, for an artist, showed an uncommon amount of practical sense and judgment. I made up my mind to enter a business college. I took a small room, ate at lunch counters, in order to economize, and pursued my studies with the zeal that I have always been able to put into any work upon which I set my heart. Yet, in spite of all my economy, when I had been at the school for several months, my funds gave out completely. I reached the point where I could not afford sufficient food for each day. In this plight, I was glad to get, through one of the teachers, a job as an ordinary clerk in a downtown wholesale house. I did my work faithfully, and received a raise of salary before I expected it. I even managed to save a little money out of my modest earnings. In fact, I began then to contract the money fever, which later took strong possession of me. I kept my eyes open, watching for a chance to better my condition. It finally came in the form of a position with a house which was at the time establishing a South American department. My knowledge of Spanish was, of course, the principal cause of my good luck; and it did more for me; it placed me where the other clerks were practically put out of competition with me. I was not slow in taking advantage of the opportunity to make myself indispensable to the firm.

What an interesting and absorbing game is money making! After each deposit at my savings-bank, I used to sit and figure out, all over again, my principal and interest, and make calculations on what the increase would be in such and such time. Out of this I derived a great deal of pleasure. I denied myself as much as possible in order to swell my savings. Even so much as I enjoyed smoking, I limited myself to an occasional cigar, and that was generally of a variety which in my old days at the "Club" was known as a "Henry Mud." Drinking I cut out altogether, but that was no great sacrifice.

The day on which I was able to figure up $1,000.00 marked an epoch in my life. And this was not because I had never before had money. In my gambling days and while I was with my "millionaire" I handled sums running high up into the hundreds; but they had come to me like fairy god-mother's gifts, and at a time when my conception of money was that it was made only to spend. Here, on the other hand, was a thousand dollars which I had earned by days of honest and patient work, a thousand dollars which I had carefully watched grow from the first dollar; and I experienced, in owning them, a pride and satisfaction which to me was an entirely new sensation. As my capital went over the thousand dollar mark, I was puzzled to know what to do with it, how to put it to the most advantageous use. I turned down first one scheme and then another, as though they had been devised for the sole purpose of gobbling up my money. I finally listened to a friend who advised me to put all I had in New York real estate; and under his guidance I took equity in a piece of property on which stood a rickety old tenement-house. I did not regret following this friend's advice, for in something like six months I disposed of my equity for more than double my investment. From that time on I devoted myself to the study of New York real estate, and watched for opportunities to make similar investments. In spite of two or three speculations which did not turn out well, I have been remarkably successful. To-day I am the owner and part-owner of several flat-houses.

I have changed my place of employment four times since returning to New York, and each change has been a decided advancement. Concerning the position which I now hold, I shall say nothing except that it pays extremely well.

As my outlook on the world grew brighter, I began to mingle in the social circles of the men with whom I came in contact; and gradually, by a process of elimination, I reached a grade of society of no small degree of culture. My appearance was always good and my ability to play on the piano, especially ragtime, which was then at the height of its vogue, made me a welcome guest. The anomaly of my social position often appealed strongly to my sense of humor. I frequently smiled inwardly at some remark not altogether complimentary to people of color; and more than once I felt like declaiming, "I am a colored man. Do I not disprove the theory that one drop of Negro blood renders a man unfit?" Many a night when I returned to my room after an enjoyable evening, I laughed heartily over what struck me as the capital joke I was playing.

Then I met her, and what I had regarded as a joke was gradually changed into the most serious question of my life. I first saw her at a musical which was given one evening at a house to which I was frequently invited. I did not notice her among the other guests before she came forward and sang two sad little songs. When she began I was out in the hallway where many of the men were gathered; but with the first few notes I crowded with others into the doorway to see who the singer was. When I saw the girl, the surprise which I had felt at the first sound of her voice was heightened; she was almost tall and quite slender, with lustrous yellow hair and eyes so blue as to appear almost black. She was as white as a lily, and she was dressed in white. Indeed, she seemed to me the most dazzlingly white thing I had ever seen. But it was not her delicate beauty which attracted me most; it was her voice, a voice which made one wonder how tones of such passionate color could come from so fragile a body.

I determined that when the programme was over I would seek an introduction to her; but at the moment, instead of being the easy man of the world, I became again the bashful boy of fourteen, and my courage failed me. I contented myself with hovering as near her as politeness would permit; near enough to hear her voice, which in conversation was low, yet thrilling, like the deeper middle tones of a flute. I watched the men gather around her talking and laughing in an easy manner, and wondered how it was possible for them to do it. But destiny, my special destiny, was at work. I was standing near, talking with affected gayety to several young ladies, who, however, must have remarked my preoccupation; for my second sense of hearing was alert to what was being said by the group of which the girl in white was the center, when I heard her say, "I think his playing of Chopin is exquisite." And one of my friends in the group replied, "You haven't met him? Allow me—" then turning to me, "Old man, when you have a moment I wish you to meet Miss ——." I don't know what she said to me or what I said to her. I can remember that I tried to be clever, and experienced a growing conviction that I was making myself appear more and more idiotic. I am certain, too, that, in spite of my Italian-like complexion, I was as red as a beet.

Instead of taking the car I walked home. I needed the air and exercise as a sort of sedative. I am not sure whether my troubled condition of mind was due to the fact that I had been struck by love or to the feeling that I had made a bad impression upon her.

As the weeks went by, and when I had met her several more times, I came to know that I was seriously in love; and then began for me days of worry, for I had more than the usual doubts and fears of a young man in love to contend with.

Up to this time I had assumed and played my rôle as a white man with a certain degree of nonchalance, a carelessness as to the outcome, which made the whole thing more amusing to me than serious; but now I ceased to regard "being a white man" as a sort of practical joke. My acting had called for mere external effects. Now I began to doubt my ability to play the part. I watched her to see if she was scrutinizing me, to see if she was looking for anything in me which made me differ from the other men she knew. In place of an old inward feeling of superiority over many of my friends, I began to doubt myself. I began even to wonder if I really was like the men I associated with; if there was not, after all, an indefinable something which marked a difference.

But, in spite of my doubts and timidity, my affair progressed; and I finally felt sufficiently encouraged to decide to ask her to marry me. Then began the hardest struggle of my life, whether to ask her to marry me under false colors or to tell her the whole truth. My sense of what was exigent made me feel there was no necessity of saying anything; but my inborn sense of honor rebelled at even indirect deception in this case. But however much I moralized on the question, I found it more and more difficult to reach the point of confession. The dread that I might lose her took possession of me each time I sought to speak, and rendered it impossible for me to do so. That moral courage requires more than physical courage is no mere poetic fancy. I am sure I would have found it easier to take the place of a gladiator, no matter how fierce the Numidian lion, than to tell that slender girl that I had Negro blood in my veins. The fact which I had at times wished to cry out, I now wished to hide forever.

During this time we were drawn together a great deal by the mutual bond of music. She loved to hear me play Chopin, and was herself far from being a poor performer of his compositions. I think I carried her every new song that was published which I thought suitable to her voice, and played the accompaniment for her. Over these songs we were like two innocent children with new toys. She had never been anything but innocent; but my innocence was a transformation wrought by my love for her, love which melted away my cynicism and whitened my sullied soul and gave me back the wholesome dreams of my boyhood. There is nothing better in all the world that a man can do for his moral welfare than to love a good woman.

My artistic temperament also underwent an awakening. I spent many hours at my piano, playing over old and new composers. I also wrote several little pieces in a more or less Chopinesque style, which I dedicated to her. And so the weeks and months went by. Often words of love trembled on my lips, but I dared not utter them, because I knew they would have to be followed by other words which I had not the courage to frame. There might have been some other woman in my set with whom I could have fallen in love and asked to marry me without a word of explanation; but the more I knew this girl, the less could I find it in my heart to deceive her. And yet, in spite of this specter that was constantly looming up before me, I could never have believed that life held such happiness as was contained in those dream days of love.

One Saturday afternoon, in early June, I was coming up Fifth Avenue, and at the corner of Twenty-third Street I met her. She had been shopping. We stopped to chat for a moment, and I suggested that we spend half an hour at the Eden Musée. We were standing leaning on the rail in front of a group of figures, more interested in what we had to say to each other than in the group, when my attention became fixed upon a man who stood at my side studying his catalogue. It took me only an instant to recognize in him my old friend "Shiny." My first impulse was to change my position at once. As quick as a flash I considered all the risks I might run in speaking to him, and most especially the delicate question of introducing him to her. I must confess that in my embarrassment and confusion I felt small and mean. But before I could decide what to do he looked around at me and, after an instant, said, "Pardon me; but isn't this——?" The nobler part in me responded to the sound of his voice, and I took his hand in a hearty clasp. Whatever fears I had felt were quickly banished, for he seemed, at a glance, to divine my situation, and let drop no word that would have aroused suspicion as to the truth. With a slight misgiving I presented him to her, and was again relieved of fear. She received the introduction in her usual gracious manner, and without the least hesitancy or embarrassment joined in the conversation. An amusing part about the introduction was that I was upon the point of introducing him as "Shiny," and stammered a second or two before I could recall his name. We chatted for some fifteen minutes. He was spending his vacation North, with the intention of doing four or six weeks' work in one of the summer schools; he was also going to take a bride back with him in the fall. He asked me about myself, but in so diplomatic a way that I found no difficulty in answering him. The polish of his language and the unpedantic manner in which he revealed his culture greatly impressed her; and after we had left the Musée she showed it by questioning me about him. I was surprised at the amount of interest a refined black man could arouse. Even after changes in the conversation she reverted several times to the subject of "Shiny." Whether it was more than mere curiosity I could not tell; but I was convinced that she herself knew very little about prejudice.

Just why it should have done so I do not know; but somehow the "Shiny" incident gave me encouragement and confidence to cast the die of my fate; but I reasoned that since I wanted to marry her only, and since it concerned her alone, I would divulge my secret to no one else, not even her parents.

One evening, a few days afterwards, at her home, we were going over some new songs and compositions, when she asked me, as she often did, to play the "13th Nocturne." When I began she drew a chair near to my right, and sat leaning with her elbow on the end of the piano, her chin resting on her hand, and her eyes reflecting the emotions which the music awoke in her. An impulse which I could not control rushed over me, a wave of exaltation, the music under my fingers sank almost to a whisper, and calling her for the first time by her Christian name, but without daring to look at her, I said, "I love you, I love you, I love you." My fingers were trembling, so that I ceased playing. I felt her hand creep to mine, and when I looked at her her eyes were glistening with tears. I understood, and could scarcely resist the longing to take her in my arms; but I remembered, remembered that which has been the sacrificial altar of so much happiness—Duty; and bending over her hand in mine, I said, "Yes, I love you; but there is something more, too, that I must tell you." Then I told her, in what words I do not know, the truth. I felt her hand grow cold, and when I looked up she was gazing at me with a wild, fixed stare as though I was some object she had never seen. Under the strange light in her eyes I felt that I was growing black and thick-featured and crimp-haired. She appeared not to have comprehended what I had said. Her lips trembled and she attempted to say something to me; but the words stuck in her throat. Then dropping her head on the piano she began to weep with great sobs that shook her frail body. I tried to console her, and blurted out incoherent words of love; but this seemed only to increase her distress, and when I left her she was still weeping.

When I got into the street I felt very much as I did the night after meeting my father and sister at the opera in Paris, even a similar desperate inclination to get drunk; but my self-control was stronger. This was the only time in my life that I ever felt absolute regret at being colored, that I cursed the drops of African blood in my veins, and wished that I were really white. When I reached my rooms I sat and smoked several cigars while I tried to think out the significance of what had occurred. I reviewed the whole history of our acquaintance, recalled each smile she had given me, each word she had said to me that nourished my hope. I went over the scene we had just gone through, trying to draw from it what was in my favor and what was against me. I was rewarded by feeling confident that she loved me, but I could not estimate what was the effect upon her of my confession. At last, nervous and unhappy, I wrote her a letter, which I dropped into the mail-box before going to bed, in which I said:

"I understand, understand even better than you, and so I suffer even more than you. But why should either of us suffer for what neither of us is to blame? If there is any blame, it belongs to me, and I can only make the old, yet strongest plea that can be offered, I love you; and I know that my love, my great love, infinitely overbalances that blame, and blots it out. What is it that stands in the way of our happiness? It is not what you feel or what I feel; it is not what you are or what I am. It is what others feel and are. But, oh! is that a fair price? In all the endeavors and struggles of life, in all our strivings and longings there is only one thing worth seeking, only one thing worth winning, and that is love. It is not always found; but when it is, there is nothing in all the world for which it can be profitably exchanged."

The second morning after, I received a note from her which stated briefly that she was going up in New Hampshire to spend the summer with relatives there. She made no reference to what had passed between us; nor did she say exactly when she would leave the city. The note contained no single word that gave me any clue to her feelings. I could only gather hope from the fact that she had written at all. On the same evening, with a degree of trepidation which rendered me almost frightened, I went to her house.

I met her mother, who told me that she had left for the country that very afternoon. Her mother treated me in her usual pleasant manner, which fact greatly reassured me; and I left the house with a vague sense of hope stirring in my breast, which sprang from the conviction that she had not yet divulged my secret. But that hope did not remain with me long. I waited one, two, three weeks, nervously examining my mail every day, looking for some word from her. All of the letters received by me seemed so insignificant, so worthless, because there was none from her. The slight buoyancy of spirit which I had felt gradually dissolved into gloomy heartsickness. I became preoccupied, I lost appetite, lost sleep, and lost ambition. Several of my friends intimated to me that perhaps I was working too hard.

She stayed away the whole summer. I did not go to the house, but saw her father at various times, and he was as friendly as ever. Even after I knew that she was back in town I did not go to see her. I determined to wait for some word or sign. I had finally taken refuge and comfort in my pride, pride which, I suppose, I came by naturally enough.

The first time I saw her after her return was one night at the theater. She and her mother sat in company with a young man whom, I knew slightly, not many seats away from me. Never did she appear more beautiful; and yet, it may have been my fancy, she seemed a trifle paler and there was a suggestion of haggardness in her countenance. But that only heightened her beauty; the very delicacy of her charm melted down the strength of my pride. My situation made me feel weak and powerless, like a man trying with his bare hands to break the iron bars of his prison cell. When the performance was over I hurried out and placed myself where, unobserved, I could see her as she passed out. The haughtiness of spirit in which I had sought relief was all gone, and I was willing and ready to undergo any humiliation.

Shortly afterward we met at a progressive card party, and during the evening we were thrown together at one of the tables as partners. This was really our first meeting since the eventful night at her house. Strangely enough, in spite of our mutual nervousness, we won every trick of the game, and one of our opponents jokingly quoted the old saw, "Lucky at cards, unlucky in love." Our eyes met, and I am sure that in the momentary glance my whole soul went out to her in one great plea. She lowered her eyes and uttered a nervous little laugh. During the rest of the game I fully merited the unexpressed and expressed abuse of my various partners; for my eyes followed her wherever she was, and I played whatever card my fingers happened to touch.

Later in the evening she went to the piano and began to play very softly, as to herself, the opening bars of the 13th Nocturne. I felt that the psychic moment of my life had come, a moment which if lost could never be called back; and, in as careless a manner as I could assume, I sauntered over to the piano and stood almost bending over her. She continued playing; but, in a voice that was almost a whisper, she called me by my Christian name and said, "I love you, I love you, I love you." I took her place at the piano and played the Nocturne in a manner that silenced the chatter of the company both in and out of the room; involuntarily closing it with the major triad.

We were married the following spring, and went to Europe for several months. It was a double joy for me to be in France again under such conditions.

First there came to us a little girl, with hair and eyes dark like mine, but who is growing to have ways like her mother. Two years later there came a boy, who has my temperament, but is fair like his mother, a little golden-headed god, a face and head that would have delighted the heart of an old Italian master. And this boy, with his mother's eyes and features, occupies an inner sanctuary of my heart; for it was for him that she gave all; and that is the second sacred sorrow of my life.

The few years of our married life were supremely happy, and, perhaps she was even happier than I; for after our marriage, in spite of all the wealth of her love which she lavished upon me, there came a new dread to haunt me, a dread which I cannot explain and which was unfounded, but one that never left me. I was in constant fear that she would discover in me some shortcoming which she would unconsciously attribute to my blood rather than to a failing of human nature. But no cloud ever came to mar our life together; her loss to me is irreparable. My children need a mother's care, but I shall never marry again. It is to my children that I have devoted my life. I no longer have the same fear for myself of my secret being found out; for since my wife's death I have gradually dropped out of social life; but there is nothing I would not suffer to keep the "brand" from being placed upon them.

It is difficult for me to analyze my feelings concerning my present position in the world. Sometimes it seems to me that I have never really been a Negro, that I have been only a privileged spectator of their inner life; at other times I feel that I have been a coward, a deserter, and I am possessed by a strange longing for my mother's people.

Several years ago I attended a great meeting in the interest of Hampton Institute at Carnegie Hall. The Hampton students sang the old songs and awoke memories that left me sad. Among the speakers were R. C. Ogden, Ex-Ambassador Choate, and Mark Twain; but the greatest interest of the audience was centered in Booker T. Washington; and not because he so much surpassed the others in eloquence, but because of what he represented with so much earnestness and faith. And it is this that all of that small but gallant band of colored men who are publicly fighting the cause of their race have behind them. Even those who oppose them know that these men have the eternal principles of right on their side, and they will be victors even though they should go down in defeat. Beside them I feel small and selfish. I am an ordinarily successful white man who has made a little money. They are men who are making history and a race. I, too, might have taken part in a work so glorious.

My love for my children makes me glad that I am what I am, and keeps me from desiring to be otherwise; and yet, when I sometimes open a little box in which I still keep my fast yellowing manuscripts, the only tangible remnants of a vanished dream, a dead ambition, a sacrificed talent, I cannot repress the thought, that, after all, I have chosen the lesser part, that I have sold my birthright for a mess of pottage.

CPSIA information can be obtained
at www.ICGtesting.com
Printed in the USA
LVHW052002170920
666285LV00019B/1109

9 781604 592177